Paulcke/Dumler   Hazards in Mountaineering

HAZARDS

Paulcke/Dumler

Translated from the German by
E. Noel Bowman, F.R.G.S.

New York
Oxford University Press
1973

Daring is fine!
Reckless impetuosity is stupid!
It is therefore wise to discover and learn
from the experience of others and to match
boldness to mature consideration, ability
to good sense. True courage is shown
only by one who is fully aware of all the
consequences of his actions.

Wilhelm Paulcke

IN MOUNTAINEERING

Oxford University Press, Inc.,
200 Madison Avenue
New York, N.Y. 10016
1973

First published in Germany by
Rudolf Rother

All Rights Reserved by
Rudolf Rother, München

English translation
Copyright © 1973
Kaye & Ward Ltd

Filmset and printed in England by
Cox & Wyman Ltd,
London, Fakenham and Reading

Jacket illustration, front:
Cimone della Pala;
back: Summit cornice on the
Wetterhorn in the Bernese
Alps.

The colour illustration on
page 2 was taken from the
book *Dolomiten* by kind
permission of Ghedina of
Cortina d'Ampezzo.

The panorama of the Sexten
Dolomites was taken from the
book *Das Panorama der Alpen*
by kind permission of
Süddeutscher Verlag, Munich.
Standpoint:
Durrenstein, 2839 metres.
View towards the southeast
into the heart of the Dolomites.
From left to right:
Dreischusterspitze, Zwölfer,
Zinne group, Cadin Spitzen,
Cristallo and Monte Pelmo.

Preface

This book has a prehistory of almost a hundred years. In April 1885, Emil Zsigmondy, a twenty-four-year-old doctor of medicine and a great guideless Viennese mountaineer, so to speak laid its foundation stone. He was the first man ever to outline the hazards of mountaineering within the confines of a book. This he did very thoroughly indeed, and in those far-off days it was a completely comprehensive work. Less than six months after the appearance of the first edition, Zsigmondy fell to his death in attempting a traverse of the south face of the Meije.

The second and third editions were produced by his brother, Otto, and Ludwig Purtscheller of Salzburg. In the first decade of this century, Wilhelm Paulcke of Leipzig, who had just started at the University of Freiburg as a geologist and mineralogist, was asked to undertake a fresh edition. Paulcke accepted: 'It was a question of continuing and bringing up to date the work of a man who, as one of the noblest and most distinguished personalities of his time, exercised a decided influence upon the development of mountaineering.'

Wilhelm Paulcke produced a completely new book, comprising the fourth to the ninth editions. It was a publication of 500 pages which even today is regarded as a standard work on mountaineering hazards, although the last edition appeared as long ago as 1933. He died in Karlsruhe in September 1949 at the age of seventy-six, as the result of a stroke.

During the summer of 1969, the publishers, Rudolf Rother of Munich, asked me to undertake a new compilation of the book. I gladly accepted this offer and paid a visit to Paulcke's daughter, Frau Randi Hafner-Paulcke of Pforzheim, to discuss it with her. This genial lady entrusted me with the task of carrying on her father's work, for which I wish to express my thanks.

The contents had to be condensed and brought up to date. Whereas the science of snow, rock, ice and avalanches remained static, modern equipment and its use had changed out of all recognition during the thirty-seven years [*sic*] since the publication of the last edition of the book. Fresh knowledge had been acquired in the conquering of difficult alpine faces and the climbing of the highest peaks and a certain amount of scientific progress had been made. All this had to be taken into consideration and inserted into the work. There is a new chapter entitled 'Hazards caused by equipment'. I did not again include the chapters on the technique of rock and ice climbing, first aid and the search for buried victims of avalanches, as these are all dealt with in specialized publications (see also the Bibliography at the end of the book).

It is not my intention to present myself as a venerable grey-haired mentor as I am still too young and, besides, I have myself had to face almost every one of these hazards. I hope that, through the publication of this edition, the practical experience of many climbers will be spread as widely as possible, thereby helping to reduce the number of accidents in the mountains.

Helmut Dumler

Contents

Part of the huge Brenva face of the Mont Blanc Massif, with its menacing hanging glaciers, between which are sited the various climbing routes.

Introduction

The Alps, like all high mountain ranges, in the very multiplicity of their formations embody a variety of hazards for climbers. The steepness of the terrain, its formation, the height of the mountains, their attendant climatic characteristics and their consequences, are the main causes of mountaineering hazards. They derive from physical and chemical changes and in the main are due to the reaction between the envelope of air (atmosphere) and the solid ground (lithosphere). Water plays an important part here, in its various forms, such as rain, mist, snow and ice. Mountain hazards have been subdivided for over a hundred years. For example, Edward Whymper spoke of positive and negative, and Julius Meurer of elementary and personal hazards. Both wished to express what Emil Zsigmondy called objective and subjective hazards. Despite the diverse nomenclature of these hazards, Zsigmondy's definition is as applicable today as it was in his time.

An example of subjective hazards, i.e. hazards caused by the climber himself. In this case it is an example of unsuitable equipment.

Objective hazards

These hazards originate from the nature of the mountain (rock, ice, snow, weather, stonefall, avalanches, etc.) rather than from the climber himself (fatigue, inadequate technical ability, etc. — see below).

The sole protection against objective hazards is the observation and understanding of these natural phenomena, combined with suitable equipment and meticulous belaying tactics. The associated theories of geophysics (science of the physical properties of the terrestrial body), of meteorology (science of weather and climate), of glaciology (science of the formation of ice and glaciers), of geology (science of the history of the formation of the earth), are all of vital importance for survival on the mountains, although they are apt to be regarded as antiquated dogma by many mountaineers.

Subjective hazards

These hazards emanate from the mountaineer and his spiritual and bodily shortcomings, such as: overestimation of his powers of orientation, of his capacity of observation and of his knowledge of elementary alpine experience, combined with lack of efficiency and underestimation of difficulties or overestimation of his own skill. The right choice of a climbing companion is also of supreme importance.

Whereas purely objective hazards are the same for every mountaineer, subjective hazards vary according to the individual. They can, however, be reduced to a minimum or eliminated altogether by resolute self-control.

Interaction of objective and subjective hazards

Wilhelm Paulcke called these 'causative hazards'. He included in this category all accidents which, according to Fritz Schmitt, were due to a succession of objective and subjective hazards. For example, the onset of a storm (objective) can very easily result in fatality if combined with incorrect procedure and deficient equipment (subjective), whereas an accident could be avoided by timely abandonment of the climb or by a bivouac with proper protection against the weather.

It will be seen that mountaineering hazards cannot be regarded as isolated incidents as it is a fact that most climbing accidents are due to the combined effects of objective and subjective dangers. Accidents caused by pure objective hazards are comparatively rare. It is therefore necessary to study at length the scene of action and the type of activity.

There are, as yet, no special regulations for mountaineering. Nobody is required to produce a certificate of experience or capability, as is the case in the USSR. This, therefore, should be sufficient reason for a certain amount of self-control to be exercised before setting out on a mountaineering expedition, which will not become a great occasion until one feels capable of undertaking it, even under adverse conditions, without vanity or misplaced ambition.

Hazards in rock climbing

Structure of a mountain

1 Summit
2 Overhang
3 Rib
4 Overhanging roof
5 Ledge
6 Top of buttress
7 Recess
8 Gap
9 Crag
10 Pinnacle
11 Breach
12 Arête
13 Edge of buttress
14 Tower (gendarme)
15 Crack
16 Chockstone
17 Chimney
18 Groove (dièdre)
19 Terrace
20 Platform
21 Cliff
22 Escarpment
23 Gully

The elevation and image of peaks and mountain massifs are so manifold that one is led to believe that any accurate and detailed structure is not possible. It is not necessary to be a geologist to know that the Alps were formed by a process of folding and thrusting which caused enormous areas of pressure and friction. Friable rock masses were shattered or ground down by overfolding and then more or less agglomerated again. This is often revealed by fine veins or cracks in the rock surface, frequently filled out by quartz, limestone spar or other material, and which point to a lack of internal cohesion. Water and ice, cold and heat, storm and weathering, all disintegrate the mountain block, furrow and grind down the rock surface. Continually operating forces, such as weathering or erosion, work incessantly on the existing massifs. In this manner, the image of the mountain world of the present day has been evolved. The subsequent ice age also had enormous influence on the relief of the Alps.

The actual nature of the rocks was and is of decisive influence upon the delicacy of their formation. Hans Hintermeier divided these rocks into three parts:

Magmatic rocks

(igneous rock, crystalline massifs) These include granite, porphyry and basalt.

Deposited rocks

(sedimentary) Of interest to the climber are limestone, dolomite, chalk, nagelfluh, loess and marl.

Metamorphic rocks

Those of most interest to the climber are gneiss, mica schist and early slate (phyllite).

Climbing on iron-hard granite.
Aiguille du Midi, south face (Rebuffat route).

Types of rock formation
Characteristics and hazards

Granite
The most widely distributed plutonic rock and also the most reliable is the old granite (protogine) which is found in the Mont Blanc massif or in the Dauphiné. This rock is characterized by knife-edged arêtes crowned with gendarmes (Chamonix Aiguilles), very steep, holdless, but firm and rough slabs (west face of the Dru) in which vertical cracks and chimneys often afford natural routes (Knubel crack on the Grépon). Features such as these have been formed by lateral pressure, producing a parallel structure. The same applies to mountains formed of younger granite, such as the Piz Badile in the Val Bregaglia.

Owing to the firmness and solidity of nearly all magmatic rocks there is little danger of stonefall when climbing in granite.

By reason of the fine crystalline structure, the rough surface permits good friction climbing. This sort of climbing can, however, exact more energy than is the case with limestone or dolomite. On high-grade climbs it is advisable to take along special section pitons and wooden wedges, as existing cracks are often too wide for ordinary pitons.

Projections, so prevalent on granite faces, frequently cause difficulty in hauling up rucksacks, and the sharp edges hinder the recovery of abseil ropes.

Schists

These are mostly three- and four-edged pyramids in the central massifs (Zermatt Weisshorn), formed of crystalline schists and

Limestone rock with last remnants of snow. Owing to the heat of the rock, a dangerous cavity has formed between rock and snow.

Abseiling in the Dolomites. (Grosse Zinne, north face, direct.) Projections and ledges, typical of the Zinne faces.

Schists. The sloping or 'roof-side' of the mountain is to the left, and the steep side to the right.

gneiss. It is not possible to form a general opinion on this type of rock as it consists of rocks of varied origins. It can just as easily be firm as friable. For example, in the Silvretta or in the Ötztal mountains one encounters solid reliable rock adjacent to extremely friable formations. It makes very little difference whether one climbs on mica schist (Täschhorn-Teufelsgrat), on talc, chlorite or green schist – they are nearly always friable. Gneiss is the only exception to this rule.

Particularly friable places in gneiss can be recognized by the reddish colour of the rock. Cracks and gullies are often full of smooth schistous debris. Care must be taken not to start a stonefall when pulling in the rope.

Care should be exercised to avoid cuts on the sharp rock. Ridges are preferable for ascent and descent rather than walls or faces. Always carry long pitons.

Limestone and dolomite

Limestones are generally divided into two types, block limestone (i.e. south face of the Marmolata) and stratified limestone such as the north face of the Hochvogel. The former rarely weathers but the latter provides soft or easily soluble material which is carried away leaving firm rock affording good holds.

Generally speaking, limestone and dolomite can be considered as reliable. Exceptions to this are ferruginous rock, recognizable by its yellow or red hue (i.e. south face of the Tofana above the Amphitheatre), and limestone which has been subjected to excessive pressure and disintegration.

Fissures and erosion chimneys are readily transformed into waterfalls after heavy rain. If at all possible, a bivouac should never be sited in a couloir or chimney, even if the weather seems fine. Limestone containing clay or loam can become very greasy after rain.

Whereas ordinary pitons can be employed in the north alpine limestone, short special pitons are frequently used in dolomitic rock where occasionally small holes are encountered with crystalline formations around the edges.

The rock and its surface

The Höfats, the well known and notorious grass-covered mountain in the Allgäu range. Apart from the Schneck, it is unique.

The superficial character of the rock ranges from bare rock to lichen, moss and grass to ice. Each of these substances requires a special technique and all conceal a multitude of hazards. If we disregard bare rock, dealt with in this chapter, and also snow which has a chapter all to itself, we are left with overgrown rock, grass slopes and iced or glazed rock.

Overgrown rock and grass slopes

The limestone foothills, such as the northern and southern limestone zones of the east and west Alps, the Drau chain and the Carinthian Alps, include a number of summits below the vegetation line, i.e. grassland and dwarf pine terrain. Disintegrated mantle rock collects on weathered slopes and ledges, vegetation takes root and thrives, frequently producing black topsoil.

This is the terrain much sought after by flower pickers, owing to its rich flora, and every summer there is a fresh crop of fatalities. There are various types of grass mountains. The crystalline quartz (chert) mountains of the Allgäu range, the principal summits of which are the Höfats and the Schneck, are unique of their kind. The resistant rock does not weather down to detritus but supplies good topsoil enabling compact grass cover to develop on less inclined slopes, whereas on the steeper gradients every crack, gully or ledge is filled with pockets of grass.

Hoar frost, fresh snow and saturation of the grass surface form additional hazards.

Fresh snow slips readily off the grass slopes (see 'Snow avalanches', p. 40). Incessant rainfall and heavy thaw make the grass slippery so that without the use of crampons it is practically impossible to maintain a good foothold. Moreover, pockets of turf, which are quite firm in dry conditions, break away when the topsoil is wet. Particular attention must be paid to these conditions in the spring. Continuing dry weather can also become hazardous as the soil loosens and crumbles. When the ground is frozen such terrain can be less hazardous than in the warmer months.

The stability of boulders lying on grass-covered chert slopes can be very variable, for the cracks and crevices are exposed to a continuous loosening-up process owing to penetrating vegetation and frost action.

The hazards depicted here naturally apply to all grassy terrain, but each has its own special characteristics.

In the folded chalk mountains, for example the French limestone regions, the Säntis range or the Bregenzerwald, where hard and soft strata alternate, the hard limestone beds often produce vertical cliffs, whereas the soft argillaceous beds give rise to grass ledges and terraces. The molasse mountains of the alpine foothills with their hard nagelfluh beds and marl interlays exhibit similar variations.

In the dolomite and limestone regions tufts of grass and small shrubs (e.g. dwarf pines) are to be found deep in cracks in the rocks. Every grass tuft should be carefully tested as the coherence of wide grass slopes with their roots is lacking. If your boots get dirty make sure that the soles are clean before continuing the climb. Lichen on the rock surface causes little problem in dry weather, but in wet conditions can be very dangerous.

Iced rocks

The climber must reckon with iced rocks; not only in the western Alps or in winter, but also in the eastern Alps and during the summer months. If the verglas is only thin and can be chipped off, no serious problem arises. Where the glazing is too thick, it may be necessary to use crampons. This procedure requires considerable practice before being put into operation.

The rock ices up rapidly after a shower of rain or when damp mist with falling temperature occurs.

Icy patches are sometimes encountered in the northern limestone Alps even in the autumn after a very early start, whereas verglas is naturally much more prevalent in the western Alps. Verglas can easily turn a IV-grade climb into a VI-grade one — and even make it impossible.

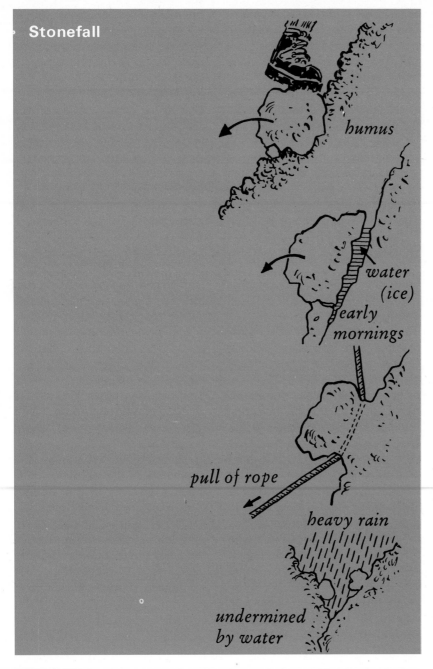

Stonefall

humus

water (ice)

early mornings

pull of rope

heavy rain

undermined by water

Causes

In the high Alps, the continual alternation of frost and heat, freezing and thawing throughout the year, plays a predominating rôle in the disintegration of the rock surface.

The radiating heat of the afternoon heats up the rock surface which cools off as the sun sinks, and at night and early morning the surface temperature frequently falls below freezing point. These temperature variations cause the rock alternately to expand and contract at different rates depending upon the type of rock and the formation of the surface as well as the rate of the change in temperature. Considerable strains and tensions are set up in the body of the rock causing cracks and clefts to appear. These tend to break up the stratum.

Rain or melted snow penetrates into the finest cracks and freezes as soon as the temperature falls. This transition from the liquid to the solid state is accompanied by an expansion of about 15 per cent which is, in effect, a wedging action, widening the cracks. So long as the frost continues, the stratum is held together by the so-called 'ice cement'. A rise in temperature causes this 'cement' to loosen with the result that if the balance of any stone is disturbed it will fall. Stonefall can also be caused by

Pitches which are subject to much stonefall are usually covered by fine rock powder and display light marks of impact which show up against the dark background.

Deep scars on névé or holes in snow indicate continual stonefall. A word of caution here: if the foot of the face is covered with deep snow, these signs will not be visible. Falling stones

often come to rest in couloirs and ice gullies and freeze in until they are released by a subsequent thaw. Scree-covered ledges buried in fresh snow, as in the Dolomites, are particularly dangerous as the stones loosen up during the heat of the day and often whole sections of the face peel off.

It is just as important to know when stonefall is likely to occur

melting snow, rain, storms and lightning, and also by animals such as chamois, sheep and choughs. Finally, the climber himself must bear some responsibility for this hazard which he can easily bring about by careless movement on loose rock.

Recognition of the hazards of stonefall

It is of primary importance to know the composition of the mountain. Rock which is subjected to much weathering, such as is the case with almost all sedimentary formations, will give rise to more stonefall than granite. Boulders and fresh rock debris at the foot of precipices (Laliderer range) and patches of scree at the outlet of couloirs and gorges all point to frequent stonefall. Such gullies are the natural collecting channels for any rock falling from the face above.

Laliderewand. This is more than just stonefall, it is a real rock avalanche, with devastating effect.

Distinguishing the hazards of stonefall:
1. Typical gully subject to stonefall, but not as dangerous as 2. Both gullies should be avoided. Safest line of ascent is the right-hand rib under 3. Faces under 4 and 5 are weathered and shattered, as is the ridge.

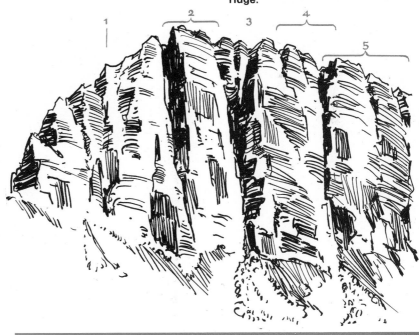

as to be able to recognize its outward traces. In the alpine foothills (northern and southern limestone Alps) the hazards of stonefall are at their maximum in late spring when the thaw is at its height.

In the central and western Alps, on the other hand, this hazard is postponed until late summer, depending upon the altitude. Increased danger of stonefall occurs during the autumn when the night frost is preceded by heavy rain.

Stonefall usually occurs early in the day on east and south faces as the first rays of the sun warm up the upper part of the moun-

This pretty girl, Helga Lindner, is wearing a crash helmet as a protection against falling stones.

It should, however, be worn lower down on the forehead.

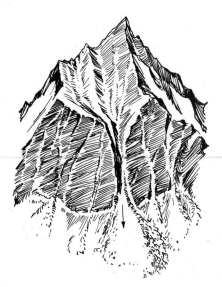

Gully subject to falling stones on a gneiss mountain. Funnel-shaped catchment area and scree cone.

tain. West and north faces, on the other hand, are usually exempt from this danger until late afternoon.

There is, however, no rule without an exception! I experienced falling ice early one summer morning at the start of the Comici route on the Grosse Zinne, and later on, stonefall.

Precautionary measures

A famous mountaineer once said that hazards and difficulties are there to be overcome. There is a world of truth in this, but basically it is better to evade the hazard by avoiding terrain exposed to stonefall or postpone the climb until a more propitious occasion.

Areas where stonefall is prevalent should be tackled at the most suitable time of day. Dangerous pitches should be avoided if a change in the weather is imminent.

Couloirs and chimneys are especially dangerous as it is impossible to foresee the trajectory of the 'missile'. Wherever possible, ridges, arêtes and outstanding buttresses should be followed. When roping-up at the start of a climb, rucksacks etc., should be stowed away in a safe place. Bivouacs or rest places must be sited in areas free from stonefall, i.e. in dead ground (under overhangs etc.).

Be careful not to frighten animals

The couloir below the west face of the Dru is a notorious track of falling stones. It leads to the start of the Southwest Pillar and west face climbs. Owing to the presence of snow, the objective hazards are somewhat diminished.

which might cause stonefall.

And now to a great source of stonefall—man! Zsigmondy once said: 'By scree shall you recognize the climber!' These words of wisdom are still applicable even in these days of screw pitons and bivouac hammocks. Careful walking, even on the roughest scree, should be just as much a part of the climber's curriculum as the overcoming of the greatest difficulties.

Roped parties should as far as possible be close together when crossing scree and the leader should warn the other members of the presence of loose rock.

Stones detached by the foot should be stopped before they fall.

It is often not possible to avoid moving stones with the rope, but this should be an exception rather than the rule.

Following parties should be given early warning of possible stonefall.

Great care must be taken in hauling up sacks or pulling down the rope after abseiling. The latter operation should take place under cover wherever possible.

Avoid tracks at the base of faces.

Behaviour during stonefall

A first principle is that a helmet should always be worn, for not only is it an effective means of protection against falling stones, but it can also protect the head

from injury in the case of a fall or even an apparently harmless slip on snow or ice.

If stonefall is likely, the climber should never feel 'ashamed' to knock in a piton even in free climbing, for in the case of a fall the height of fall will be diminished or impact with rock may be prevented. Warning should be given of stonefall by shouting. Thoughtless behaviour, such as clinging to the smooth face, is a natural reaction but is wrong if only a few small stones are involved.

Isolated stones should be evaded at the last moment if the climber is unprotected and the stance and belay permit.

In the case of a salvo of stones or a rock avalanche, take cover as soon as possible under an overhang, a protruding rock, in a recess or in dead ground.

If the stonefall is continuous, the pitch must be climbed as quickly as possible, preferably in rushes between salvoes.

When the stonefall is over, the rope must always be inspected for possible damage.

Even on faces free from falling stones (east face of the Grand Capucin), a helmet should be worn as it will protect the skull in case of a fall.

A fall on rock

The assumption that falls occur only on extremely severe vertical and overhanging rock faces is wrong. In actual fact it is quite possible to fall on any slope where a slip can occur.

Causes

There are many causes for a fall on rock. Very often it is due to inattention (stumbling), which occurs frequently through over-tiredness, carrying too heavy a sack, bad light or adverse weather conditions.

When climbing, the causes can range from breaking of equipment (pitons or wooden wedges) or the coming away of a hold, which in most cases is the fault of the climber (i.e. insufficient testing of holds), to stonefall, lightning or overestimation of one's competence. Once more we come up against objective and subjective hazards, but, generally speaking, most accidents are due to incorrect performance on the part of the climber.

Preventative measures

The first rule is 'do not fall', which presupposes a perfect mastery of the art of climbing. It is, moreover, almost always possible in any terrain to provide additional belaying points (running belays) which reduce the height of fall, since the climber will fall twice the distance between himself and a running

Ascent on a fixed rope by means of jumars. The Prusik technique is too exhausting for a long ascent and scarcely practicable, especially after a fall.

belay rather than twice the distance from the second man. Although this sometimes makes the rope more difficult to manœuvre, especially on traverses, the increase in safety makes it well worth while.

Conduct during the fall

If the fall takes place on sloping terrain, or on grass slopes or broken rocks, it depends solely upon the climber whether what starts as a simple slip is immediately arrested or whether he falls backwards and rolls over. He must at once try to turn over onto his stomach with his legs hanging down the slope, while endeavouring at the same time to brake with hands and toes.

There has been much theorizing about falls on vertical and overhanging rock. In the latter case the fall is free and is not likely to cause much injury, but with a fall on vertical ground there is always the danger of impact with the rock face. In this case it has been suggested that the climber should thrust himself away from the face. I regard this as pure theory which would be possible only if the fall was foreseen.

My own reactions in the case of an unforeseen fall would range from raising the arms to the head to protect my face as far as possible, to grasping the rope or scrabbling with the fingers on the rock surface. This would lead to badly torn finger-tips, hardly a prerequisite for further safe climbing.

If the fall takes place on sloping or vertical terrain in the direct fall line of the belaying leader, not much harm will be done provided, of course, that he is paying attention and is belaying correctly. If, on the other hand, the fall occurs on a traverse, the consequences can be extremely serious both for the leader and the second man. If the leader has not belayed himself onto a high-sited piton at the commencement of the traverse and comes off, he will fall and swing, whereas if the second man comes off he will 'only' swing, unless he has also belayed himself before he starts on the traverse. The natural reaction of the 'swinger' is to stretch forward his arms and legs, which is about the only self-protection he can have.

Conduct after the fall

It does not lie within the scope of this book to deal with first aid. There are plenty of professional publications on this subject. Every climber should have some knowledge of first aid and also know the Alpine Distress Signals, which are as follows:

Signal A visible or audible signal given at regular intervals six times in the minute.

These should be repeated after a minute's silence until a reply is received.

Reply A similar signal given at regular intervals, three times in the minute.

Most falls on vertical or overhanging terrain without projecting rocks take place without incident, apart from the fall itself, but the situation immediately afterwards can become extremely serious.

If the second man cannot help the fallen climber by lowering him onto a projection or pulling him up, he will be obliged to help himself as quickly as he can, particularly if he is not wearing a climbing belt, unless he is badly injured. If he is not equipped with a climbing belt the constriction of the rope around the body will paralyse the arms within half an hour. Anyone hanging free on the rope for more than two hours is usually finished. This can be avoided only by the use of a combination of climbing belt and harness, which would enable a climber to hang free on the rope for hours without coming to any harm.

Many have scoffed at this equipment and climbed without it — and died. Why do glider pilots always wear a parachute when flying over land, when they are rarely likely to use it? It is a

Prusik knot on rope. The long loop can be either under tension or unweighted.

The Mountain Rescue Service bringing down a climber with a head wound with a steel cable.

regulation; mountaineers have no such regulations, only advice.

If one is hanging free on the rope, the first thing to do is to relieve the strain of the rope round the chest immediately. For this purpose a foot loop or étrier should be carried, easily ready to hand. It is obvious that perfect mastery of this technique is necessary (Prusik knot, jumars, etc.) and should be well practised beforehand. This technique is also used in mountain rescue work.

Immediately following the accident, the belayed second man must hold the fallen climber — thus the mastery of belaying tactics is self-evident. Fortunately, over the last few years a variety of new methods of belaying has been evolved. The reader may well ask which is the most reliable. Christoph Herrschel, the Munich belaying expert, gives the answer: 'The best method of belaying is one which in any given set of objective and subjective conditions presents the least possibility of risk.' In other words, one should be familiar with all types of belays.

Snow, cornices and avalanches

A precise study of snow — the nature of its deposition and, in particular, the changes which it undergoes — has been neglected for much too long. The researches and publications of Wilhelm Paulcke have brought some light into this darkness. He was one of the first who ventured into the winter mountain fastnesses on skis. In the meantime, numerous scientific and popular publications on this subject have appeared. Any list of these must include the works of Walther Flaig, Albert Gayl, Hans Hintermeier, Sepp Islitzer, Leo Krasser and Melchior Schild.

Anyone venturing into the mountains in the winter must be familiar with the characteristics of snow and its attendant hazards, for he bears a great responsibility not only to himself but also towards his companions.

Forty years ago, Wilhelm Paulcke said: 'Instead of letting loose vast hordes into the mountains through the medium of ski and mountain climbing schools, thereby transforming them into mountaineers (?) and alpine ski runners, it would be better if the leaders of these enterprises paid more attention to the dangers inherent in these sports.' This statement was made at a time when the present-day scale of piste ski-running was still a dream of the future. Nevertheless, his words are entirely applicable today and still do not seem to have made much impression. There is little doubt, however, that warnings on the radio and in the press during the winter months have borne some fruit. Despite this, during the winter of 1969–70 there were sixteen reported fatal avalanche accidents in North Tirol alone. Fifty-six persons were buried, thirteen of whom died. The depths at which they were buried varied from just under the surface to 18 feet, but of these only three were lower than 6 feet. According to statistics (Sepp Islitzer), seven of the sixteen died as a result of their own carelessness.

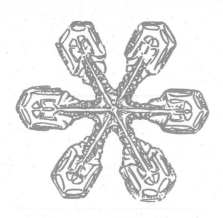

What is the origin of snow?

Snow occurs at low temperatures by the transition of moisture in the air into the solid state. This takes various forms:

Snow crystals These occur either in the form of small hexagonal columns and simple hexagonal plates (which crystallize and grow slowly at very low temperatures and under scarcity of water vapour) or as large, more-or-less dendritic stars with six rays (which form at high temperatures with an abundance of water vapour). At temperatures around freezing point the stars cohere and hook together forming snow flakes.

Soft hail This consists of snow crystals which have turned into hoar-frost pellets by the attachment of super-cooled fog droplets.

Hail This occurs when soft hail pellets fall through layers of air saturated with moisture, much

below freezing point.

Frost This is formed by the deposition of super-cooled water vapour from the air onto super-cooled objects. Considerable deposits of frost can occur on old snow beds making a powdered or loose surface especially good for skiers.

Hoar frost This is a feathery deposit of quick-freezing super-cooled fog droplets formed in gusty wind conditions. It always extends against the direction of the prevailing wind and is therefore important for orientation purposes.

What is the weight of snow?

A cubic metre (about 35 cubic feet) of freshly fallen powder snow weighs between 30 and 60 kg. When the snow settles and if it is subjected to any change in composition, the weight can increase to between 200 and 600 kg (wet snow). Wet firn (névé) can increase in weight up to 800 kg. This is considerably more than half a ton and one can well understand how even a small avalanche can enclose a body as in concrete.

The principal types of snow and their characteristics

New snow – powder snow

This consists of freshly fallen snow, not more than twenty-four hours old, the original crystalline formation of which can still be seen. It is divided by Paulcke into dry and wet new snow.

Dry new snow

This may be subdivided into powder snow, farinaceous snow, surface hoar and wind-packed snow. Dry new snow does not ball up in the hand and at low temperatures remains loose for a long time on shaded slopes and at great heights when there is no wind. If there is a good under-

layer of old snow, it makes for good skiing. Wind-packed snow, on the other hand, makes skiing difficult.

Wet new snow
This is heavier and balls up easily in the hand. It clogs under skis, on boot soles and between the crampon points. It falls at temperatures close to freezing point and is apt to change to powder snow after frost.

Old snow – settled snow
This is formed of snow granules changed into snow crystals and older than twenty-four hours. This 'firnification' process, due to external causes, transforms the snow into a granular mass, producing firn snow.

Firn snow – old snow
Composed of various types of granulation, firmly frozen together. Wet firn becomes more mobile with increasing humidity, thus forming a basis for wet old snow avalanches. Old snow is excellent material for building bivouacs.

Crusted snow
This ensues from the superficial melting and regelation of coarse granulated crust. When the sun is shining it forms on the sunny side, while powder snow is present in the shade. When crusted snow breaks under the skis it is called breakable crust. On slopes which are exposed to strong sunlight during the day, the surface crust becomes superficially soft (firn snow). If this softening-up process is very intense, avalanches can fall throughout the night, following a slight frost, and may well continue until the old snow bed has hardened.

Depth hoar
This is another variation of old snow, which does not ball up, and compared to the usual structure is very light and mobile. Depth hoar strata constitute excellent gliding surfaces and if there is a hollow space under the surface an avalanche may occur.

Metamorphosis of snow

The properties of the snow are changed. This has a considerable bearing on the formation of avalanches.

Changes from above
These are mostly due to atmospheric influences such as temperature, sun, rain, wind, etc. The original star formation of the snow crystals does not remain for long as evaporation and new formations set in at once. Even at low temperatures soon very little remains of the delicate dendritic structure. Larger surfaces are formed which reflect the light, so that the frozen new snow glitters. This is the light and fluffy powder snow.

Moreover, at very low temperatures minute granules form on

the branches of the snow stars, and before long only granules having a very loose structure are visible. At higher temperatures (solar radiation and the like) the friability of the particles decreases. Evaporation alternates with the formation of new granules and thaw water is produced. The hollows due to thaw decrease in size as the snow becomes heavier through its moisture content and sets. This is wet snow which can produce wet snow avalanches.

The older the snow becomes, the greater is the formation of granules; the smaller granules evaporate and the subsequent water vapour assists the growth of larger ones. Melting and freezing processes constantly alternate and firnification proceeds apace. Layers of crusted snow, composed of coarser firn particles, form on the surface between pauses in snowfall, particularly when the sun is shining.

During the latter part of the winter, a number of heterogeneous layers with sharply defined boundaries are formed on the surface in this way, each to be buried in its turn below the next layer of new snow, which itself eventually acquires a firm top surface.

Changes below

Far-reaching recrystallization takes place in the surface snow which is not visible to the eye. According to tests made by Paulcke, the ground temperature below a deep layer of snow is of the order of +0·5 °C. Water vapour is formed which is cooled by the snow and other external sources, resulting in abundant crystallization. Paulcke has called the final product 'depth hoar'. The formation of depth hoar proceeds upwards towards the surface in zones in which water vapour is present – Paulcke has come across layers of over 3 feet in depth.

While the formation of firn crystals within the snow progresses from exterior to interior, the formation of depth hoar crystals increases in the inverse direction until, at the end of the winter, both types meet each other. According to Albert Gayl, this formation of depth hoar in the interior usually occurs only during frost conditions, particularly during periods of extended frost.

Snow sections

This book is written for the practical climber and this chapter is especially dedicated to the touring ski runner and winter mountaineer who leaves the hut during the night and sets out for a summit. Certain aspects must be discussed which may cause some people to smile but which, nevertheless, can be of vital importance. Among these is numbered the snow section which indicates the existing layers of snow.

While it is not a practicable proposition to keep on cutting snow sections in the course of an expedition, it is definitely worth while devoting a little time to this operation on an off day or if one is held up by bad weather.

How to make a snow section
A trench should be dug right down through the snow layers to ground level. It will then be possible to evaluate the different strata and their boundaries. The section should then be brushed

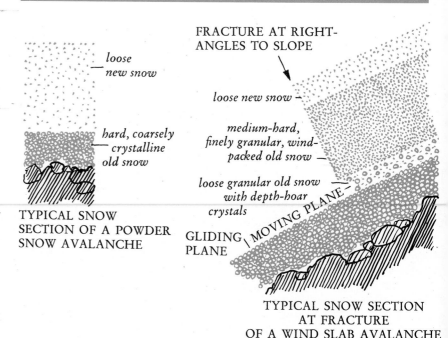

loose
new snow

hard, coarsely
crystalline
old snow

TYPICAL SNOW
SECTION OF A POWDER
SNOW AVALANCHE

FRACTURE AT RIGHT-
ANGLES TO SLOPE

loose new snow

medium-hard,
finely granular, wind-
packed old snow

loose granular old snow
with depth-hoar
crystals

GLIDING
PLANE

MOVING PLANE

TYPICAL SNOW SECTION
AT FRACTURE
OF A WIND SLAB AVALANCHE

with a hand broom in the direction of the various layers so that the harder strata stand out. The different types of snow can then be determined for research purposes with the aid of a microscope or a pocket magnifying lens.

How to evaluate a snow section

If a master snow section has been cut and theoretically resolved — a knowledge of the snow structure being essential — the next step is to make a sounding to test for feel and audibility. A sounding stick is necessary for this operation and these can be procured in collapsible pocket-size. A ski stick can also be used for this purpose. For example: the stick penetrates the top layer of new snow by its own weight. It then encounters a layer of crusted snow, a definite resistance can be felt and the penetration no longer continues. The firmer the crusted snow layer is, the more difficult it will be to penetrate; also the striking tone of the sounding stick is harsher. If, on the other hand, the stick meets ice, a clearer note is produced. When fine-grained firn snow is encountered a grinding or scraping noise is heard. This type of snow can even be felt with the disc of a ski stick, whereas with powder snow and depth hoar hardly anything is felt or heard.

Wind and snow

Snow rarely falls in a state of absolute calm, i.e. snowfall is usually accompanied by storm and wind. The thickness of the snow bed very rarely corresponds to the average amount of fallen snow.

What do snow plumes indicate?

Often during a snowfall and even after it has stopped snow is blown by wind from the windward to the lee side of a mountain. In this manner the summit areas in particular are denuded of snow which accumulates in vast quantities on the lee side, mostly in hollows or depressions. Even on very clear sunny days huge snow plumes are to be seen on crests and ridges.

These plumes indicate that the lee slopes are deep in loose snow and prone to avalanches; there is also the local danger of wind slab formation.

Cavities

A cavity is formed when snow, driven by the wind, meets an obstacle such as a tree or boulder. A pressure area occurs on the windward side and an eddy-pool on the lee, which prevents any deposition of snow. In fact, the eddies actually scoop out the snow, up to a depth of about 6 feet. A cavity like this would form a good basis for a snow-hole bivouac.

Snow cushions

These are small localized accumulations of powder snow, situated below ribs, ridges and humps, and especially at breaks in slopes. They are particularly prone to avalanches.

Sastrugi

These are continuous ridges or hummocks formed by wind erosion of wind-pressed snow, and should not be confused with 'snow dunes' which are accumulations of wind-driven snow with gentle weather sides and steep lee sides. Their steep sides are directed towards the wind whereas their lee sides are more level.

What is a wind slab?

If the pressure of the wind on the snow is unusually strong, huge coherent layers or slabs are formed.

It is often the practice to refer to superficially not very extensive avalanches as wind slabs, which, according to Paulcke, is incorrect as all avalanches start off as layers or layer complexes with

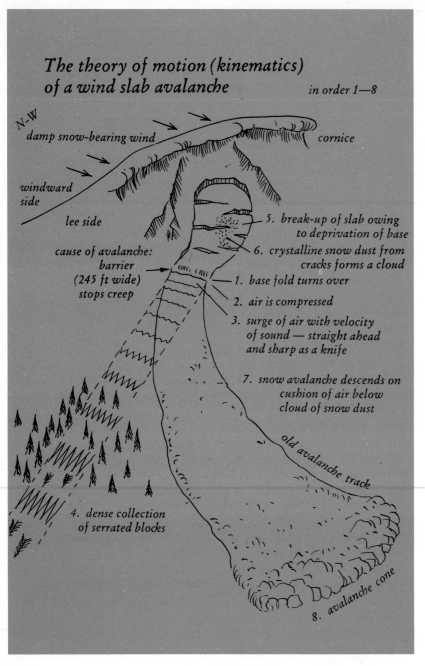

The theory of motion (kinematics) of a wind slab avalanche

in order 1—8

N-W

damp snow-bearing wind

cornice

windward side

lee side

cause of avalanche: barrier (245 ft wide) stops creep

5. break-up of slab owing to deprivation of base

6. crystalline snow dust from cracks forms a cloud

1. base fold turns over

2. air is compressed

3. surge of air with velocity of sound — straight ahead and sharp as a knife

7. snow avalanche descends on cushion of air below cloud of snow dust

old avalanche track

4. dense collection of serrated blocks

8. avalanche cone

sharply defined lines of fracture. Wind slab avalanches may be of limited scope but can also cover wide slopes. There are also wind slabs of a voluminous slab-like nature right down to a hard underlayer which may consist of crusted snow, firn, ice, rock or grass.

A wind slab is formed by the perpetual drifting and wind-packing of snow. Others are formed by the upper layer of a mass of powder snow being wind-packed into a slab, while the underlying snow remains loose and powdery. There are also many other transitional forms.

If depth hoar is present under a wind slab, acute danger of avalanches is to be expected.

Wind slab is treacherous in that its hard surface lulls one into a false sense of security. The inexperienced mountaineer believes himself to be on a solid underlayer whereas in reality he is standing on an extremely unstable slope. As he cannot make any impression on the hard surface with his skis, he stamps hard and digs in his edges thereby making an indentation on the slab which is under extreme tension. In consequence, the tension is released and the slab breaks away (usually above the ski track) with a loud crack, splits into sharp-edged blocks and thunders down to the valley as a wind slab avalanche.

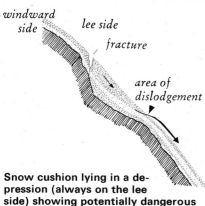

windward side   *lee side*
fracture

area of dislodgement

Snow cushion lying in a depression (always on the lee side) showing potentially dangerous area of dislodgement at its lower end.

Above:
Typical fracture of a wind slab, sharply defined and perpendicular.

Right:
Track of an avalanched wind slab.

Below right:
A dry wind slab avalanche (settled snow avalanche). Worth noting is the break across the slope (under tension).

Below:
Termination of a wind slab avalanche, shortly after its start.

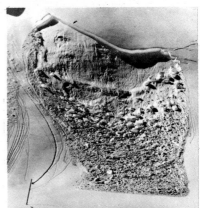

33

Cornices

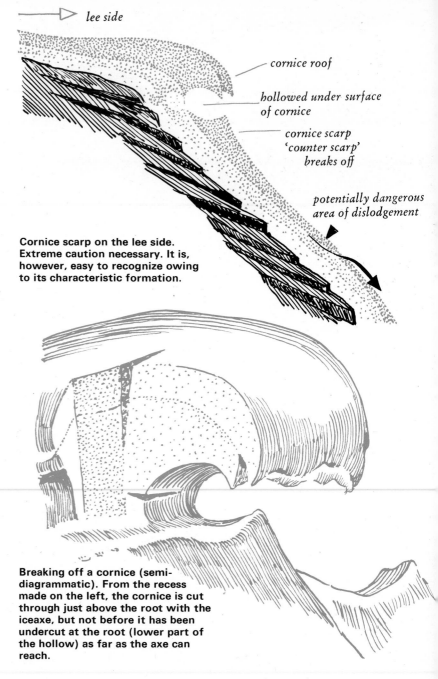

lee side

cornice roof

hollowed under surface
of cornice

cornice scarp
'counter scarp'
breaks off

potentially dangerous
area of dislodgement

Cornice scarp on the lee side. Extreme caution necessary. It is, however, easy to recognize owing to its characteristic formation.

Breaking off a cornice (semi-diagrammatic). From the recess made on the left, the cornice is cut through just above the root with the iceaxe, but not before it has been undercut at the root (lower part of the hollow) as far as the axe can reach.

These are roof-like overhanging snow formations which owe their origin to the deposition of snow by the wind. They build out over crests and ridges. There are two types of cornices: suction and pressure cornices. They are, in addition, subdivided into winter and permanent cornices according to the time of year, and into ridge and plateau cornices.

Suction cornices

Their formation is approximately as follows: the air stream flows towards the windward side of the ridge, rising to the crest and carrying with it snow particles. These particles flow over the crest and come to rest on the lee side. This is the basic form of the suction cornice.

Pressure cornices

A prerequisite for the formation of pressure cornices is when the surface of the cornice reaches

Winter cornice on the Kleinglockner.
The climber is dangerously near
to the eventual point of fracture.

the air stream-line, owing to the continuing development of the suction effect. The snow particles, carried by the wind, drive over the surface of the snow and give place to a tighter cohesion produced by the grains being pressed together by the wind.

Winter cornices

These are formed during the winter snowfall and occur mostly in the lower alpine regions of the central Alps. Winter cornices naturally do not exhibit any very solid formation and are perpetually sinking so that the ideal stream-line is frequently not attained. During a fall of snow this leads to the formation of fresh, superimposed suction cornices.

Permanent cornices

In the Alps this type of cornice usually forms only above about 3000 metres. The formation of this type of cornice is similar to that of the winter cornices.

Due to the long-lasting action of heat and cold, wind and its own dead weight, the permanent cornice becomes so strong in the course of time that very little sinking action takes place, so that the danger of breaking away is much less than with winter cornices.

Ridge cornices

If a ridge descends steeply on the windward side and much less steeply on the lee side, two conditions obtain. Firstly, there is no catchment area capable of supplying snow for deposition by the wind — in fact, snowfall plays practically no part in the formation of these cornices — and secondly, the energy of the wind beating against the steep flank is nullified by the formation of eddies. Thus, the wind is not able to transport the snow particles to the lee side and deposits them on the ridge.

On ridges the conditions for the formation of cornices are much more favourable when the wind blows from the less steep side. If the gradient on the windward side is extremely steep, the eddying is so great that a cornice will probably not form on the lee side.

Plateau cornices

A plateau cornice is formed as follows: the flatter a slope or plateau, the more uninterruptedly can the wind blow across the surface of the snow, carrying along with it particles of snow and building up a cornice in the dead ground directly behind the ridge.

Cornices and their hazards

Cornices can become very dangerous for the climber if they are stepped on or if they fall down

On a ridge like this (Mont Maudit) it is best to keep to the crest.

Descent from the summit of Schchara in the Caucasus. The party in the foreground is at the limit of safety and should not be so close together.

along the upward route.

The danger of permanent cornices breaking off on their own without human intervention in the summer is comparatively small. Winter cornices, on the other hand, are not very solid and have little resistance, so that they can quite easily break off, particularly during a thaw or a storm.

Where the angle eases off at the edge of a corniced ridge, the mountaineer is occasionally tempted to step on the cornice itself, which is often difficult to recognize from the windward side.

Every climber should realize that a cornice does not break away right at the overhanging portion but usually farther back (see sketch on p. 38). Visual evidence of the presence of a cornice is often provided by the discovery of a thin dark line of junction running parallel to the crest of the

conjectural point of fracture
possible point of fracture
track →

windward
side

lee side

Ascent from Col Marzell to the summit. The dangerous cornice area is readily seen on the upper part of the arête.

ridge. Another fact to remember is that avalanches are quite liable to be set off in the winter, and after fresh snowfall in the summer, by a falling cornice.

How to cope with cornice hazards

Those who know how many famous climbers (e.g. Fritz Kasparek, Hermann Buhl, etc.) have fallen to their deaths by the breaking off of cornices will not underestimate the dangers inherent in cornices and will act accordingly.

It is of paramount importance that the party should be roped and that the distance between members should be sufficient for only one man to be upon the corniced part of the ridge at any one time.

The roof of the cornice should be avoided at all costs. A sufficient margin of safety from the likely breaking point should be maintained, even if it involves descending the slope and cutting steps.

Even if a track is seen traversing the danger zone which a former party has successfully negotiated, the climbers should proceed on their own, safer, way. Gullies should not be used for an ascent if crowned by a cornice.

How to surmount cornices

It often occurs that when climbing up or down a face, a cornice has to be surmounted. It may also on occasion be necessary to beat down a cornice from above in order to get through to the line of descent.

From above

After careful inspection from the side from a projection of the ridge, a notch should be cut at a point where the cornice roof is at its narrowest. The first man (suitably belayed) will climb

38

through the hole in the cornice and take up a good belaying position below and to the side, so that the second man can follow.

From below

In this situation also, a place should be chosen where the projecting cornice is at its narrowest. A position to the side of the eventual exit should be adopted before the first man attempts to hack through the cornice or climb over it.

It is a dangerous practice to tunnel through a cornice and attempt to climb out in this way as the root area of the cornice will be disturbed, and it is not always possible to judge from below the distribution of weight at the sinking point of the cornice.

What to do if a cornice falls

If the belaying second man has not got a good stance and is not tied on, there is only one thing to do if the leader falls owing to the breaking of a cornice: jump down the other side of the ridge. This is not just an idle theory, for many climbers have done just this and thereby saved their own lives and that of the fallen man.

Summit of ridge cornice on the Egelseehörndl in the Salzburg mountains, showing a pronounced crescent-shaped hollow.

Snow avalanches

In order to be able to form an accurate opinion of the presence of threatening avalanche conditions, it is necessary to have at one's finger-tips a profound knowledge of the characteristics of the snow already described. There is a variety of causes of avalanches, such as deposition of snow by the wind, overloading of lee slopes, wind slab formation, soaking of the snow surface, variations in the snow surface and freezing of the top layer. The summer mountaineer should take a good look at the snow-free slopes and compare the map with the actual topography if he wishes to form a clear opinion of likely avalanches in the winter. Each and every slope should be carefully examined with regard to its gradient, its homogeneity, the inclination of the declivity of the slope or its interruption by terraces, the dissemination of boulders, the structure of the rock under the snow and the type and thickness of vegetation.

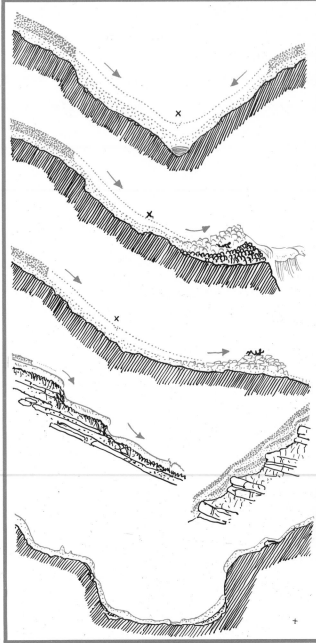

Narrow V-shaped valley without formation of a valley floor. Danger of avalanches from both sides.

Slope above a glacier. Avalanche was released by disturbance at × and came to rest on the moraine below.

The snow layer was disturbed at × and avalanched down into the valley. It was able to run out on the slope and the cone was therefore shallower.

Left: Outward-dipping strata with steep drops. Very prone to avalanches. Right: So long as the terrace formation supports the snow, there is little danger from avalanches.

Wide, trough-like glacier valley (V-valley) with terraces and valley bottom safe from avalanches.

How snow avalanches are started

They begin when the equilibrium of the snow layers is disturbed, either by the dead weight of the snow causing it to slide or by external causes which release the internal cohesion of the snow stratum.

Wide valley basin with gentle slopes and a flat valley bottom with terrace formation. No danger from avalanches on the valley floor.

When do snow avalanches start?

The determining angle can as a rule be considered as about 24 degrees. In the case of very smooth underlayers (smooth slabs, ice-polished rocks, tufts of grass) or underlying crusted snow, the starting-point can be as low as 17–20 degrees. A gradient of between 30 and 40 degrees is particularly dangerous. The threat of avalanches increases where the uniform drop of the slope extends over a wide area. In such cases, any movement of the snow must be treated as a minor avalanche or snow slip which might build up into a bigger one.

Terraces and breaks in the slope are partially levelled out during the course of the winter, so that slopes, which even after fresh falls of snow in the early winter do not exhibit signs of avalanche threat, can be very dangerous later on. Avalanches are much more likely to start on a slope where the strata dip outwards

Dry powder snow avalanche. It started on its own just below the ridge and was released lower down by skiers.

Powder snow avalanche in the Swiss mountains. Although this type of avalanche normally occurs in winter, it can take place at any time of the year under cold conditions, especially high up.

than on one where outcropping rocks would hold up a slide.

The nomenclature of snow avalanches

According to Albert Gayl's book on avalanches, this is as follows:

1. That part of the slope where the snow layer was fractured, i.e. the starting-point of the avalanche, is known as the 'fracture area'. Its upper edge is the 'line of fracture'.
2. That part of the slope followed by the avalanche is the 'avalanche track'.
3. The end of the avalanche where the moving snow masses come to rest is the 'avalanche cone'.

Classification of avalanches and their effects

There are two basic types of avalanches: new snow (also powder snow) avalanches and old snow (also settled snow) avalanches. As will be seen, these are subdivided under different headings.

New snow avalanches

These consist of snow fallen within the last twenty-four hours of which only the topmost layer is involved. The snow has no internal cohesion and is not consolidated with the underlying surface.

Nevertheless, the threat of an avalanche is not imminent even after a heavy fall of snow in still air. As long as the snow remains powdery and falls back into the footprints made in a track, there is still no cohesion between the layers. The most destructive form of the dry new snow category is the powder snow avalanche; it is capable of destroying whole forests and villages. It is to all intents and purposes a winter avalanche but can occur at any time after a cold spell, especially in the higher Alps.

This avalanche threat can persist for a comparatively long period after heavy snowfalls, the greatest danger coming on the first fine day. New snow avalanches pulverize to a very high degree on falling, giving rise to considerable danger of suffocation. Damage to the lungs can be caused by atmospheric pressure, or the victim can be sucked into an eddy and thrown through the air.

Dry wind slab avalanches

These are formed of dry snow or of snow from earlier snowfalls which has remained in powder

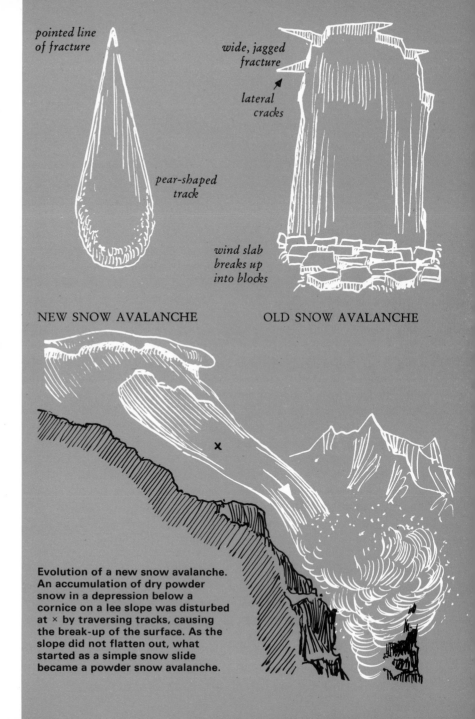

pointed line of fracture

pear-shaped track

wide, jagged fracture

lateral cracks

wind slab breaks up into blocks

NEW SNOW AVALANCHE

OLD SNOW AVALANCHE

Evolution of a new snow avalanche. An accumulation of dry powder snow in a depression below a cornice on a lee slope was disturbed at × by traversing tracks, causing the break-up of the surface. As the slope did not flatten out, what started as a simple snow slide became a powder snow avalanche.

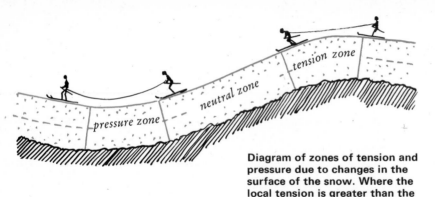

Diagram of zones of tension and pressure due to changes in the surface of the snow. Where the local tension is greater than the solidity of the snow layer, the surface will crack or break.

form over a long period and has been packed by agency of the wind. One of the most formidable of recent times was the 'Zugspitze Avalanche' on 15 May 1965, which killed ten and injured twenty-three persons.

Wind slab is always a local phenomenon and prevails when wind packing takes place under the influence of general or localized air streams. Wind slab, which is always dangerous even when the slope appears perfectly safe, fractures with a loud crack and slides down the slope in block formation. If the avalanche run is steep it usually pulverizes en route.

Wet new snow avalanches

These consist of damp or wet snow emanating from the last snowfall at higher temperatures (snowflakes), from prolonged rain or föhn or strong solar radiation after the fall. Slopes covered with powder snow of older consistency are also dangerous if it is saturated with thaw water onto which the wet new snow falls.

Although wet new snow avalanches do occur in winter, they are typical products of the spring and after snowfalls in the summer.

The avalanche flows more slowly at the edges and the base than in the centre and on the surface.

There is always the danger of being deeply buried, when death would supervene by suffocation owing to lack of oxygen and forcible compression of the body by the packed snow.

Dry old snow avalanches

Wilhelm Paulcke also designated these as 'depth hoar avalanches' because of a thin crust of depth hoar supporting the overlying snow mass. If stepped on, the snow stratum lying above the depth hoar breaks with a loud 'wuum' and rushes, hissing, down the slope.

If it appears desirable to rope up (e.g. because there is a cliff below which the avalanche would go over), the party should do so at long intervals as this type of avalanche is usually very wide in extent.

Wet old snow avalanches

Also known as firn snow avalanches, consisting of everything lying on the slope, i.e. the layer of old snow, ice, rock, grass, etc., they require no external aid to set them off and almost always fall of their own accord.

They are particularly liable to fall in the spring under föhn conditions or in rainy weather. The melting process causes the firn grains to move against each other, the lubrication medium being supplied by water.

Wet old snow avalanches do not produce snow dust but freeze solid in constricted pressure areas and in the avalanche cone.

Powder snow avalanche on the Schwarzmönch (Bernese Alps). A photograph can give only an impression of its devastating force. Mountaineers caught in one like this would be irretrievably lost.

A summary of the avalanche prevention and warning system

In the 1940s and 1950s the Swiss radically altered their existing system of avalanche prevention. They changed over from the construction of solid defences, such as tunnels or galleries, and introduced a system of interlinked protective works with a view to preventing the whole slope from peeling off in its entirety. The Confederation became the leading nation in the fight against the dangers of avalanches. In 1931, the Federal Commission for Snow and Avalanche Research was founded, and in 1942 the Federal Institute for Snow and Avalanche Research was built on the Weissfluhjoch (2660 metres) near Davos. It is financed by the State and today has a staff of thirty. Apart from a general study of snow conditions and suggestions on how to prevent avalanches by means of structural operations, it has established a Warning Service. Twenty-five years later, the Austrians followed suit and founded in Bregenz the Institute for Applied Geology, Snow and Avalanche Research. This institute operates in collaboration with the German Avalanche Warning Service on the Zugspitze.

Reports from the institute, announced in the press and on radio, should invariably be taken into consideration when planning a tour. Attention should also be paid to warnings given by hut guardians, foresters, wood cutters, etc., as they are usually very well versed in local snow conditions.

The descent is 'officially closed' and must be avoided at all costs.

Prevention is better than . . .

First golden rule: Do not undertake any mountain expedition if a sudden change in the weather appears imminent; never start if the föhn is blowing or during or immediately after a fall of new snow. Do not set foot on steep lee slopes, especially during changeable weather or during or after strong solar radiation.

If wind and temperature conditions during the last few days are unknown, it is advisable to judge the safety of the snow by digging a snow section.

The time of day is of great importance in the elimination of the avalanche danger. For example, a south-facing slope can be quite safe in the early morning, but very dangerous in hot sunshine, and a few hours later when the sun is off the slope, quite safe again.

When choosing a route through a narrow valley the following rules are worthy of note: on cold winter days proceed along the foot of the warmer slopes, and on hot spring days below shady colder slopes. Anybody who makes a careful study of weather conditions, nature of the ground, the conditions of the snow surface, etc., will soon realize that the avalanche problem is extremely complicated and frequently presents the mountaineer with an almost insoluble task. Every responsible climber must, however, come to grips with the situation. In many other forms of sport (if we are to include mountaineering in this category), such as flying, diving, etc., a lot of theory must be mastered before one gets down to putting it to a practical test. Is the fact that 90 per cent of winter fatalities in the mountains are caused by inexperience and carelessness not poignant enough?

Paulcke has stated that courage and a bold enterprising spirit are not enough to enable a successful expedition to be accomplished in the mountains under winter conditions. Keen observation, knowledge, experience and action based on these are what is necessary. Nothing comes home to roost more than reckless bravado in the mountains, particularly in winter.

Snow slope in late winter. The various layers of snow can be seen in the section in the foreground. The slope was disturbed at +, which, according to Paulcke, caused the snow cushion to avalanche.

One must be prepared for avalanches

Every climber must be constantly on the watch in terrain subject to avalanches. How should one behave in such circumstances?

1. In considering whether to rope up on glaciers, decide whether avalanches or crevasses present the greatest danger.

2. An avalanche cord should always be tied on in such a manner that the arrows point towards the climber. [An avalanche cord (Lawinenschnur) is a length of red line attached to and trailing free behind at least one member of the party, so that in the event of an avalanche it will show up against the snow if the climber is buried. *Translator's note*.] The carrying of an avalanche magnet is also to be recommended. They are now obtainable in many sports shops.

3. Remove wrists from ski-stick straps; only the thumb should be allowed to remain in the strap. Loosen ski safety bindings.

4. Put on all protective clothing, such as pullovers, anoraks, gloves, etc., and button up all pockets. If a dry snow avalanche appears likely, a scarf or handkerchief should be tied round nose and mouth.

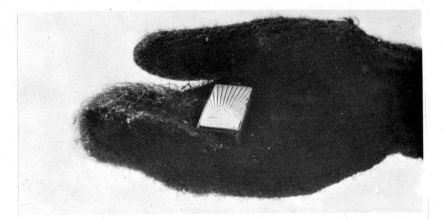

5. Be mentally prepared for the descent of an avalanche. In this manner the critical moment of surprise which has often bereft the climber of appropriate reaction may largely be averted.

6. Disturb the snow surface as little as possible. Do not edge the skis too much so as not to cut the slope.

7. However, where there is a layer of soft snow on a stable subsurface it may be safer to remove skis and travel on foot, as the foot would penetrate to the subsurface, and consolidate the track.

8. Only one person at a time on a suspect slope. As soon as he has left the danger zone, the next man should follow. If the party has a rope the last man should carry it.

9. The most important task of the alpine ski tourer is the choice of route. Any natural obstacles to an avalanche such as trees, boulders, levelling-off of the ground, should be utilized, even if this means making a detour. Ridges and

A comparatively harmless snow slide which, however, could injure skiers (broken legs).

ribs provide the safest terrain. At all times the slopes above must be kept under observation.

10. Traverse a slope as high up as practicable so that only a relatively small amount of snow is above any possible line of fracture.

11. If powder snow is lying superimposed on old snow, it is advisable to remove skis and ascend or descend in the fall line. The foot must penetrate right through to the layer of old snow so that both layers remain coherent.

12. In misty conditions with a top layer of new snow, it is often difficult accurately to judge the snow condition and the formation of the slope (gradient, length, etc.). Sounding as well as accurate reading of the map are then indispensable. In cloud etc., the rear man should take hold of the avalanche cord of the man in front.

13. As far as the snow conditions permit, the upward track should be used for the descent, especially in misty weather.

14. Never place reliance upon an existing track. In the first place, tracks are often inexpertly sited, and in the second place what was safe some time ago may be dangerous now.

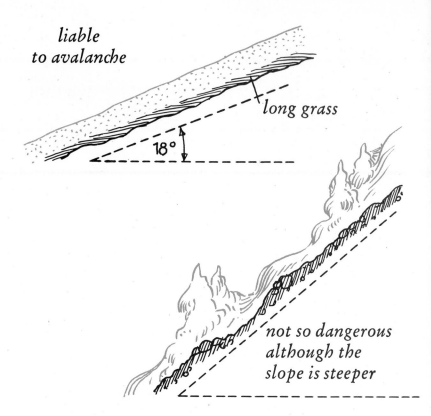

liable to avalanche

long grass

18°

not so dangerous although the slope is steeper

Tactics during an avalanche

If caught in an avalanche, rapid and appropriate reaction will diminish the danger.

Reference may be made here to the avalanche disaster at Lenzerheide on 14 March 1968. One of those buried was rescued safe and sound after nearly five hours under the snow; he said that by heavy and incessant breathing he was able to form a hollow space of over 2 feet above him in the snow.

1. If an avalanche has broken loose above, the skier should 'schuss' down the slope (if not wearing skins) or run out to the side of the avalanche track.

2. If one happens to be close to the line of fracture at the time of the avalanche, it may be possible to hang onto shrubs or the like.

3. There is no escape from a

powder snow avalanche. Crouching down or hanging onto some object may prevent the climber from being sucked off the slope and thrown through the air. If the victim is not wearing a scarf or handkerchief over nose and mouth, pressure of the mouth into the armpit will help to keep the snow dust from penetrating into the respiratory passage.

4. The first maxim on being caught in an avalanche is to take off the skis and throw away the sticks.

5. In powder snow avalanches, swimming motions help to keep the victim on the surface and, perchance, to reach the edge of the track.

6. Always try to remain upright in wet snow avalanches and avoid large blocks so as to lessen the danger of being crushed.

7. If one is buried, the arms should be crossed in front of the face and chest before the avalanche has come to a standstill, in order to maintain a breathing space.

8. The victim should try to determine his position in the avalanche. Is he the right way up or upside down? Spittle can help here as it always flows downhill. If it is at all possible to free oneself from an avalanche,

the hollow space formed by breathing is a good place to start.

9. Remain as quiet as possible and conserve the strength and breathing. Overcome the desire to sleep as this can lead to rapid death.

10. Darkness is no reason for despondency, for even under the most favourable conditions practically no light will penetrate a layer of snow a couple of feet thick.

Searching for avalanche victims with a trained dog is, despite technical devices, the most widely used method.

If the victim can hear the rescue party he must make himself heard by calling out. As I know from my own experience, it is possible to hear the barking of dogs or the sound of a car even from a depth of several yards.

Chances of survival of an avalanche victim if dug out by his own party or by an organized rescue operation.

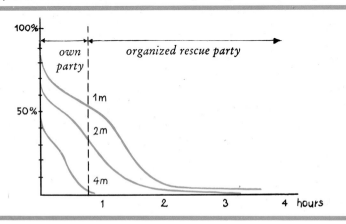

Further hazards in snow

Crevasses in rocky terrain

Rocky terrain, with large cracks or holes, when snow-covered, can be just as dangerous as crevassed firn. In many cases it is even more dangerous, as the direction of the cracks and crevices in the rock is less conformable than the general run of crevasses on glaciers.

Under conditions of deep winter snow it is quite safe to ski, but in the spring and early winter, especially after a fall of new snow, it is imperative to rope up when traversing fissured terrain.

Holes caused by melting

Caution should always be exercised at all junctions of rock and snow, particularly in the vicinity of large rocks, as melting processes often cause depressions into which one can fall. These are usually holes caused by melting due to radiation effect of the warmer rocks.

This hazard usually crops up in

the spring when boulders are situated above or just beneath the surface of the snow.

Avalanche cones

Great caution must be paid to avalanche cones, especially in the spring, as these conceal streams. If a climber falls through into one of these he is liable to be swept away. If this should happen any rescue attempt would be practically hopeless.

Glissading

Although many assert to the contrary, there is very grave risk involved in descending without skis (glissading). There are two techniques involved: a standing or a sitting glissade.

The former method is more generally practised. Apart from the experience required, the terrain must also be studied. Glissading should never be attempted if the gradient of the slope increases towards the bottom, if it is not possible to see the final run-out, if the slope is interrupted by steep sections, or unless one is certain not to encounter icy patches on which it would be difficult to halt.

Steep gullies bordered by rocks

are always dangerous, as are boulders projecting above the surface. The helmet should always be worn when glissading. Stopping: Follow the technique of the old Christiania turn, i.e. a quick body turn with a little hip movement, lateral turning of the feet and transfer of weight to the inner foot.

If an emergency stop is to be expected, carry an iceaxe (or a piton hammer in one hand and a piton in the other) so that in case of a fall the climber can turn over onto his stomach and brake accordingly.

Although a sitting glissade with the knees drawn up to the chest is pleasant, it is equally unpleasant to encounter a rock buried beneath the snow surface. While this is unlikely to cause a fatality it could give rise to serious injury. It should also be borne in mind that in a sitting glissade the clothing gets wet through.

The glissade can be brought to a halt by pressing in the heels and standing up or by forcing the shaft of the iceaxe down into the snow.

Left: Cavity caused by thawing on the Speckkarspitze in the Karwendel range; hard remains of avalanche snow which is popular for glissading.

Right: Remains of avalanche snow in the Val Savaranche; very exhausting to cross and a good example of the enormous force of a big avalanche.

Skiing and winter mountain- eering

Up until the end of the last century, most mountaineers looked upon the Alps in winter as inaccessible, even on skis which, at that time, were not regarded as a suitable aid to mountaineering. It was Wilhelm Paulcke and his companions who, just before the turn of the century, provided the indisputable proof of the usefulness of skis for mountaineers by undertaking a series of alpine ski tours, notably the traverse of the Bernese Alps.

After 1901, this outstanding example was rapidly and successfully copied. Ski touring was taken as a matter of course and today mountaineering without it would be unthinkable. Despite the great development of piste skiing, every year more and more undertake the great classic alpine ski tours such as the Haute Route from Chamonix to Saas Fee. Indeed ski running has now attained such proportions that ice and firn walls are descended which were formerly (and are still today) regarded as difficult ice routes. Examples of this are the northwest face of the Wiesbachhorn, east face of Monte Rosa, northwest face of the Aiguille de Bionassay, etc. These achievements, however, are only for the few specialists and will remain so in the future. Nevertheless, 'off-piste skiing', as Paulcke called it, will become increasingly popular.

Wilhelm Paulcke: He who undertakes to lead a skiing party in the mountains must know the Alps in summer, be a safe climber on ice or glaciers and have a profound knowledge of snow and weather conditions.

This is not the place to discuss technique and equipment of alpine ski running. It is self-evident that a much higher degree of mastery of the skis is required for ski touring than for ordinary piste skiing. Literature on skiing has increased to an enormous extent in recent times. Fortunately, the development in technique has increased enormously, especially through the study of the mechanics of movement of the body and skis, as well as by the use of slow-motion and ordinary films.

Ski touring in Canton Valais (High Level Route); the Matterhorn, with the Dent d'Hérens to its left.

Correctly sited track of ascent. It avoids areas prone to avalanches and the turns are made at safe points. Where it is impossible to avoid traversing the slope, this takes place fairly high up and only one at a time. Danger spots are at 2 and 3; at 1 the main danger is past.

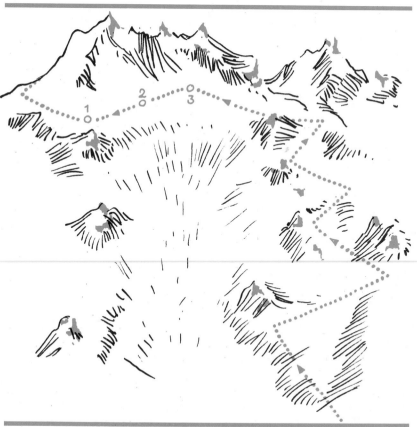

Much has already been written about the dangers of avalanches. Ski touring, however, embodies hazards which in themselves, in most cases, do not endanger life but which may be considered as a secondary source of peril. For example, the breaking of a leg in the high Alps could quite easily lead to death by freezing.

Apart from knowledge of the technique of skiing, a basic principle of successful and safe ski touring is familiarity with the nature of the snow surface. It is quite wrong to rely entirely on the bindings, for every winter there are from 80 000 to 100 000 accidents due to bindings.

According to Christof Stiebler, editor of *Winter*, if the 'Warentest' foundation, which tested twenty binding systems in the spring and summer of 1969, had maintained the original test specifications, not a single one would have earned the distinction of 'good'

Ski ascent on the Gran Paradiso.
Good equipment and clothing are
essential for ski touring.

or 'satisfactory'.

In other words, if we do not wish to run the risk of injury we must rely on our own know-how to avoid falling as far as possible. When touring in the mountains, the basic principles are endurance, self-preservation and as few falls as possible. When running downhill the rucksack should be secured by a strap round the stomach.

At least one iceaxe and one pair of crampons should be carried per party. The correct siting of a line of ascent compatible with the exigencies of the terrain, without 'zigzagging all over the place' as Paulcke puts it, and with turns at the right place, demands a certain delicate touch on the part of the skier. A word of warning: when making kick turns in heavy snow the safety bindings can quite easily open.

Frequency of injuries due to skiing.

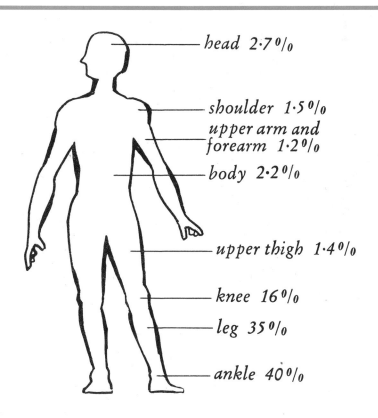

head 2·7 %

shoulder 1·5 %
upper arm and
forearm 1·2 %

body 2·2 %

upper thigh 1·4 %

knee 16 %

leg 35 %

ankle 40 %

Hazards due to the surface of the snow

The nature of the surface of the snow covering can make or mar the pleasure of skiing. Upon it depends whether the descent is worth the labour of the ascent.

An unexpected breakthrough with the ski tip, when passing from soft snow or a shaded part of the slope onto a superficially hard frozen crust, can result in a headlong fall, especially if the snow brings the ski to a sudden halt. The force of such a fall can be so severe that the foot or the knee joint can be sprained or twisted.

Changing snow conditions can terminate a 'schuss' abruptly or, on the other hand, when passing from soft snow to an icy surface, so speed it up that a fall is probable. Moral: pay attention to the snow surface when running down.

Ski descent of the northwest face of the Wiesbachhorn. This type of mountaineering is possible only under very favourable conditions and even in the future will not be suitable for the beginner.

Roped ski descent. It looks easier than it actually is. The middle man should not be tied on to the rope which runs through a karabiner attached to his harness.

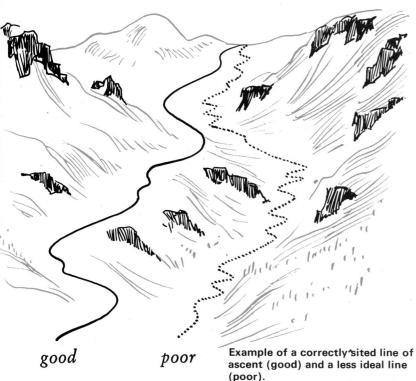

good   *poor*

Example of a correctly sited line of ascent (good) and a less ideal line (poor).

Hazards due to crevasses

Although the danger of a skier falling into a crevasse is less than that of a man on foot, skiers should always be roped up on glaciers.

In the spring, the high season for mountain ski touring, the young snow bridges caused by the action of the wind are of variable strength and usually unreliable. At this time of year the direction of the crevasse system is easier to determine than on the snow-covered glaciers of the winter months. Sharp turns on very crevassed terrain are more likely to lead to breaking-in than straight running. Braking by means of a stem turn, preferably at an angle to the line of the crevasses, provides maximum safety.

A descent over a glacier or crevassed terrain is most easily accomplished with two on a rope, separated by 20 metres, but three is safer since there is less risk of all of them being pulled into a crevasse if one goes in. The rope technique should be practised beforehand on easy terrain until perfection is attained. The best skier should be last as he has to adapt his speed to that of those in front. When there are three on a rope, the middle man is not tied on but has the rope running through a karabiner attached to his climbing belt.

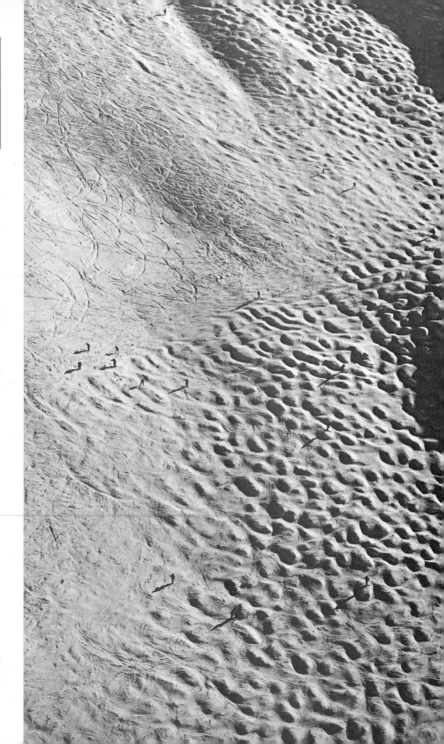

Piste skiing

The well-known Himalayan climber, Marcus Schmuck, remarked in a lecture that the construction of lifts and téléferiques 'had made it possible for the masses to ski in terrain of a partly mountainous nature'.

The alpine pistes are annually occupied by hundreds of thousands of skiers, with the result that the attendant hazards, nearly always of a subjective nature, have already become a social problem. What is the cause of piste accidents and what are the most serious dangers?

Dr W. Baumgartner, of the Surgical University Clinic in Innsbruck, interrogated 1000 victims of skiing accidents and asked them what was the principal cause. He came to the conclusion that:

20 per cent came to grief on a good piste through skiing too fast;

20 per cent owing to rotten wet snow;

15 per cent in deep virgin snow;

13 per cent on icy patches.

The remainder, 32 per cent, admitted that their downfall was due to bad edging; in other words,

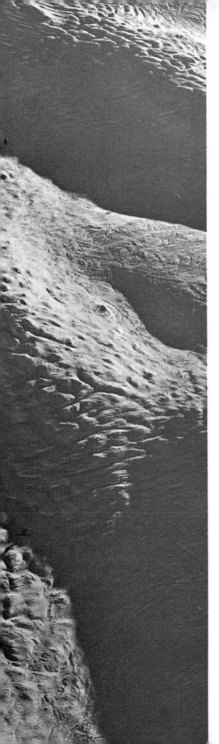

imperfect control of the skis. Avalanches can also fall on piste slopes and one should not entirely rely on the assumption that a piste will necessarily be closed when there is an avalanche threat. A personal evaluation of the condition of the terrain is essential. Naturally, closed pistes must be avoided at all costs. Piste runners should never leave the track as they are rarely suitably equipped for winter mountaineering conditions.

Although accidents on skiing pistes are generally referred to as 'sports accidents', I have nevertheless devoted a chapter to them in this book, for basically the dangers on pistes form a part of the dangers of mountaineering. When all is said and done, there are few ski tourers who do not enjoy a run down a piste from time to time or who may have to terminate a high mountain tour on a piste in order to reach the valley.

This picture clearly shows that even much-frequented tracks are not free from avalanches and are not always closed when they should have been.

Centre: Air view of a bumpy piste (Madloch run). Even popular pistes such as this one conceal hazards, but they are mostly of a subjective nature.

Close proximity of piste skiing and ski touring (ascent of the Seekareck in the Radstädter Tauern). Which is the more dangerous?

Owing to increasing overcrowding of the pistes and the numerous accidents, the FIS (Fédération Internationale de Ski) was forced to establish rules of behaviour on pistes, somewhat analogous to those in force on the roads.

Dr Josef Pichler, councillor to the Austrian Court of Appeal and an authority on skiing law, pronounced as follows: 'Anybody not obeying these rules and in consequence of which comes into collision with another skier and injures him, may be the subject of an indictment by the Public Prosecutor, and if the injured party makes a claim against him he may also be liable for damages.' Such is the situation today on alpine ski pistes. Whatever one may think about these rules of behaviour, they cannot be ignored. This is part of the nature of skiing and responsible persons will regard them as sacrosanct as the rule

of the road. Dr Pichler has supplemented the FIS rules to read as follows:

1. Selection of line of descent: The skier must take into consideration his own skill in choosing the line of descent.
2. The descending skier has precedence over the ascending skier. He must, however, look behind him before starting off to make certain that he is not impeding or endangering other skiers.
3. Controlled running: The skier must have control over his skis. He must adapt his speed to his skill, difficulty of the terrain, the condition of the snow, the visibility and the presence of other skiers.
4. The skier must always observe the terrain ahead of him and any other skiers on his descent and allow for any obstacles or obstructions. He must always be in a position to evade such obstructions or stop before

This sort of 'equipment' may be all right for the piste, but off-piste running should not be attempted in clothing like this.

he reaches them.

5. Emergency fall: If the skier cannot evade or stop before an obstacle, he must throw himself to the ground in order to avoid a collision with another skier or to diminish the force of the impact.

6. A slower preceding skier has precedence. A skier coming up fast behind a slower skier must adapt his speed to that of the latter who has precedence over the former. The skier during his descent is not obliged to turn round and regard skiers behind him.

7. Safety interval: The rearmost skier must maintain an appropriate safety interval between himself and the man in front. The same principle applies in the case of an overtaking or passing skier with regard to the skier ahead or anybody standing to one side.

8. A skier on a drag lift has precedence. Where the piste crosses the track of a drag lift, the skier under tow has precedence.

9. Road traffic has precedence over skiers. At road crossings the traffic on the road has precedence over that on the piste.

10. Dawdling on pistes: The skier must neither unnecessarily stop nor dawdle at obscured or narrow parts of the piste. A fallen skier must vacate the piste as quickly as possible.

11. Ascending skiers and pedestrians: These persons will generally use the edge of a piste for ascending.

12. Attention to signs: Skiers must pay attention to signs along the piste.

13. Use of pistes: Only skis or similar articles of winter sports equipment must be used on pistes.

14. Animals on pistes: Animals must never be allowed to run loose on pistes when skiing is in progress.

15. Accidents: Any skier in the vicinity should report his presence and lend help where necessary.

63

Winter mountaineering

Winter mountaineering is the most difficult alpine 'game'. This photograph was taken during a rescue operation on the east face of the Watzmann.

The first great winter climb in the truest sense of the word was the ascent of the Matterhorn via the Italian ridge from 16 to 17 March 1882 by the Italian Vittorio Sella, with Jean-Antoine, Louis and Baptiste Carrel as guides. Almost eighty years later, the notorious north face of the Eiger was conquered by Walter Almberger, Toni Hiebeler, Toni Kinshofer and Anderl Mannhardt from 6 to 12 March 1961, constituting a veritable *tour de force* in winter mountaineering.

Whereas summer climbing necessitates special mental and physical faculties, much more is demanded by winter mountaineering. Exertion and fatigue begin to make themselves felt even on the approach to the climb. Skis and snow shoes may have to give way to exhausting tracking even before the actual ascent can begin. Only very infrequently is a provisioned hut available as a base, and the climbers have to rely on an ice-cold refuge to which one has access only with an Alpine Club key.

On the ascent itself, one has to contend not only with the normal difficulties but also with the bitter cold and iced or snowed-up rocks, and at the same time only a few hours of daylight can be expected. A winter ascent can never be regarded as a pleasure but rather as a magnificent adventure and the best possible preparation for the most difficult climbs in the western Alps.

Basically, the steeper the rock and the more pitons found in it, the fewer additional difficulties are to be expected.

South and east faces are usually in better condition than north and west faces. The so-called 'winter ice' is more brittle than the ice usually encountered under summer conditions and, in consequence, has to be treated more circumspectly.

On winter ascents it is advisable to carry additional pitons as pitches which in summer can be surmounted without difficulty will often require extra iron-mongery under winter conditions. Extraordinary temperature variations are encountered, particularly in late winter: dazzling sunlight followed by raging icy snowstorms.

The ascent of a face has very often to be abandoned before the summit is reached; for example, we were in a narrow chimney on the south ridge of the Riffelkopf in the Wetterstein range and found the exit completely blocked by deep snow. One must always be prepared for a retreat. The short days must be used to the full and a site for

The Frenchman, René Desmaison, on the first winter ascent of the Freney Pillar in the Mont Blanc Massif. Even the approach to the face was very fatiguing and Desmaison and his companions had to make use of snow shoes (see picture).

a bivouac reconnoitred in plenty of time.

It is even more important in winter than in summer to leave behind a note stating where the party has gone and when it expects to be back in the valley. Every winter mountaineer must be a first-rate climber; a know-ledge of skiing is here of secondary importance.

If possible, at least one member of the party should have knowledge of the proposed climb under summer conditions, particularly as regards the descent which can easily present problems if difficulties should arise.

As any falling snow is usually dry, there is little danger of wetness leading to freezing. Stonefall is not to be expected and avalanches hardly ever fall on steep rock faces; nevertheless it is inadvisable to stand about for long at the foot of a climb or to have to wait overlong owing to a party in front.

Glaciers, névé and ice

High-lying basins form the catchment areas of the snow which principally falls in the winter months. Even in summer, however, the high Alps are subject to storms, periods of frost and the snowfalls which go with them. This snow is deposited in layers on the slopes and in depressions. Dependent upon the duration of the fall, its nature and any subsequent variation in the composition, these layers frequently exhibit varying degrees of thickness and structure.

After the new snow falls it sets.

On average, above the snowline more snow falls than melts. Precipitation and temperature variations gradually change the incipient loose or powder snow into firn snow. It is of passing interest to know that 20 to 26 feet of powder snow will produce about 3 feet of firn snow. The air is expelled from this by the pressure of the layers above.

Infiltration of melting snow helps to fill up the still remaining cavities. Firn ice is formed from firn snow and this in turn is transformed, mainly by pressure, into the blue or blue-green glacier ice. The transition from freshly fallen snow to glacier ice takes from 3 to 5 years.

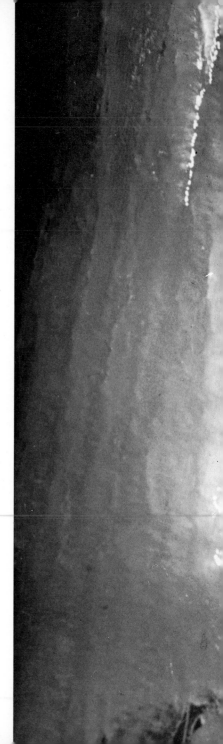

Types of glaciers and ice

Hanging glacier on the north face of the Ailefroide. Falling ice is to be expected directly under the glacier.

Valley glaciers
This term applies to most of the great glacier streams of the Alps, which have been in retreat since about 1850. No new glaciers are in course of formation.

Cirque or corrie glaciers
These glaciers are situated above the snowline in cirques or corries, e.g. the Schöllhorn glacier below the Schöllhornplatte on the east face of the Watzmann.

Plateau glaciers
Situated on tablelands. A typical example is the $3\frac{1}{2}$ sq. mile Übergossene Alm in the Berchtesgaden Alps.

Gorge glaciers
Usually fed by avalanches and situated in sunless gorges and valley floors, e.g. the Taconnaz Glacier in the Mont Blanc range.

Hanging glaciers
These cling to steep faces lying above cliffs and present a precipitous frontal section.

Brittle ice
During the summer the snow and firn melt. The greater part of the melt-water evaporates, flows away or percolates through the surface. This percolated water expedites the freezing process or freezes on the surface, forming so-called brittle ice which covers the faces with a smooth, hard veneer or fills up the cracks.

Glazed ice (verglas)
This is in complete contrast to the clear, rotten firn ice and is mostly produced by melt-water. It is usually encountered in the middle of summer or in the autumn and can immeasurably increase the difficulties of an ascent. Completely smooth ice slopes are, however, rare as there is usually a frozen firn layer on the ice.

A fascinating glimpse inside the icefall of the Waxegg Glacier. Very dangerous, although the séracs appear solid and compact.

Hummocky ice on the Glacier des Bossons in the Mont Blanc Massif. These hummocks facilitate the ascent as they provide natural holds.

69

Ice climbing

Ascent of a snow-covered glacier (Barre des Ecrins). The upper crevasse separating the glacier from the main face is clearly visible.

Willo Welzenbach, the great ice climber who perished on Nanga Parbat in 1934, wrote (in the *Alpine Handbook*) about the great differences between rock and ice climbing.

The fact that bases are far away, which increases the length of the tour, and that the prevailing climatic conditions are aggravated by the variations in height (heat, cold, lack of oxygen, etc.), means that major snow and ice routes in the high mountains can be very serious undertakings.

The rock climber knows the difficulties he has to expect and he knows the weapons of his opponent. Objective dangers, such as stonefall or storms, do not play a predominant rôle. Apart from the technical difficulties afforded by the mountain, the ice man has to do battle with a fierce army of natural forces. All this goes to show the greater competence and experience required of the ice craftsman over and above that of the pure rock gymnast.

Let us close this section with another quotation from Welzenbach: 'The explorer of the glaciated regions of the high Alps must above all things be an accomplished mountaineer.'

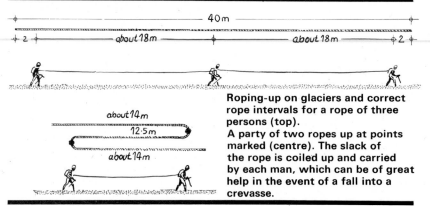

Roping-up on glaciers and correct rope intervals for a rope of three persons (top).
A party of two ropes up at points marked (centre). The slack of the rope is coiled up and carried by each man, which can be of great help in the event of a fall into a crevasse.

The glacier surface

Its features may be defined as follows:

Moraines
Debris, fallen from the bordering mountain slopes and carried down by the glacier, collects at the edges of the ice stream and forms moraine walls. The outside of the walls is firm while the side facing the glacier is loose and unstable and must be negotiated

Open glacier covered with detritus (Glacier Noire, Dauphiné).

Glacier covered with boulders and moraine debris. Very tiring to negotiate.

with care; in fact it can be unclimbable, depending upon its steepness.

Medial moraines
Formed at the confluence of two glaciers by the junction of the two inner moraines, originally the lateral moraines of the glaciers; can often be utilized with advantage as a method of ascent.
There is also the terminal moraine which is situated at the glacier tongue, and the ground moraine which is of little consequence as it does not appear before the ablation of the tongue.

Bare glacier
This zone extends from the tongue to the snowline and is largely covered with debris and streaming with water. The surface is usually rough and the crevasses are visible and can be jumped over or avoided. The rope should be used on a bare glacier in a situation where a careless step or a mistimed jump, particularly if half-asleep during a night traverse, could lead to disaster.

Snow-covered glacier
This is usually the zone which extends upwards from the snowline, which, of course, varies considerably from time to time. A rope must always be used, as the crevasses are snowed over and difficult to recognize.

Crevasses

These occur when, owing to the movement of the glacier, the forces of tension are greater than those of pressure and result in the solidity of the ice being disturbed.

Because of incomplete internal cohesion, due to the displacement of the component parts or separate layers of the ice, the accumulation of ice and névé assumes a slow gliding movement in which the force of gravity plays a predominant rôle. A glacier flows downhill like a river (the Blaueis glacier in the Hochkalter range moves at about 10 feet a year, whereas the speed of the huge Aletsch glacier in the Bernese Alps is about 330 feet) and hugs the bed of the valley.

If the tension becomes too great, the brittle ice fractures (firn ice is said to have less cohesion than glacier ice). The first sign is a fine crack on the surface, which may close up if the valley floor becomes flat again. If the gradient of the valley floor de-

Crevasse zone on the Hintereis Glacier (Ötztal mountains). These alarming-looking crevasses are relatively harmless as they are easily seen.

creases still further, the crevasses may close up, but this may be only on the surface of the glacier, forming the so-called A-type crevasses, in contrast with the normal V-type which narrow down at the bottom.

Thus crevasses are formed as a result of the movement of the ice or the substratum over which the glacier flows. The thicker the ice mass, the more the irregularities of the valley floor appear as crevasses on the surface.

72

This illustration of an icefall gives a clear indication of the formation of crevasses (Fiescher Icefall, Bernese Alps).

Transverse crevasses in the foreground, intersecting crevasses in the centre and icefalls in the background. The mountain in the distance is the Alphubel (Canton Valais).

Marginal crevasses and bergschrunds

The former are due to the radiation of heat from the rock causing the formation of a cavity between ice and rock. The latter occur when the more solid ice of the glacier breaks away from the less stable layer of ice on the walls, which is usually frozen to the bottom, or where the level trough-shaped névé basin breaks away from the steeper ice flank.

Where a glacier comes into contact with rock or an ice slope there will always be a crevasse. These crevasses are often filled up by avalanches, forming bridges. If one of these bridges falls in, fragments usually jam together but are liable to break through at a touch. These crevasses are ideal for bivouac purposes provided there is no likelihood of avalanches or stone-fall as they are less subject to change than other types of crevasse.

Transverse crevasses

They run across the main flow of the glacier but adapt themselves to the concave form of the troughs in the névé basin. They are caused by tensile stresses set up where a glacier descends over an irregularity in the valley floor. An increase in the gradient of the substratum of only 2 to 3 degrees can result in the formation of crevasses. Soundings of nearly

73

1000 feet in depth have been measured in transverse crevasses. These crevasses do not necessarily occur at the steepest part of the surface; they may be found a considerable distance higher up.

Icefalls

These have the same origin as transverse crevasses, but in this case a gradient of from 25 to 30 degrees in the valley floor is essential. The surface of the glacier is broken up into towers (séracs), ridges and needles. This zone of fracture naturally increases with the speed of flow which is greater in the centre than at the edges of the glacier.

As soon as the gradient decreases, the tensile stresses are released and the broken blocks are welded together by pressure and regelation and the glacier flows on as a coherent mass.

There is always danger of falling séracs in icefalls, particularly

Right: Chasm on a slope. If on a large scale, there is always the danger of falling through as is the case with marginal crevasses.

Left: Example of a bergschrund marginal crevasse. In the foreground is a break in the névé, and in the background the névé has separated from the rock.

with temperature rises, solar radiation, storms and the like, so that they should be circumvented or traversed rapidly.

If, on descending a glacier in bad visibility, narrow transverse crevasses are encountered which subsequently gradually become wider and deeper, one can be quite certain that an icefall is close at hand. Equally, if it is known that one is approaching an icefall, one must be prepared for transverse crevasses.

Marginal crevasses

These occur principally at the edge of a glacier as the speed of flow there is less than that at the centre. Transverse crevasses approaching the edge frequently merge into the marginal variety; naturally enough they are widest at the edge and tend to narrow as they attain the centre of the glacier, so in the case of narrow glaciers the marginal crevasses

can meet in the middle.

When walking over a glacier in bad visibility, the vicinity of the edges can usually be determined with some accuracy by the presence of such crevasses which gradually widen in one direction. The glacier is also for the most part covered with moraine debris in these areas.

Longitudinal crevasses

These are less common than the transverse type and are met with either when the glacier basin widens, thus permitting lateral expansion of the ice, or when a ridge of rocks extends along the valley floor in the flow-line of the glacier. In this manner, areas of tension are created at right-angles to the line of flow causing the ice to break up.

Intersecting crevasses

If the glacier should flow over an obstruction on the valley floor,

for instance a convex rocky protuberance falling away on all sides, tensile stresses operate in all directions leading to the formation of radial crevasses. The direction of these irregular intersecting crevasses cannot be foreseen.

Radial or fan-shaped crevasses

These are encountered at the snout of a glacier. The ice spreads out in all directions at the tongue causing crevasses to appear which run from the edge towards the middle in fan-shaped form.

If the glacier snout spreads out, longitudinal crevasses are also possible. As a rule, however, the climber will have left the glacier long before he reaches the snout. In bad visibility fan-shaped crevasses can be useful as a means of orientation or determination of one's position on the map.

Bergschrund at the bottom of the north face of the Aletschhorn (Bernese Alps). Above this are menacing hanging glaciers, especially on the left side of the face where a new snow avalanche has come down.

Bergschrund and avalanche cone at the foot of the north face of the Triolet (Mont Blanc range) after a fall of new snow.

Radial crevasses on the Lower Theodul Glacier. Icefalls and a hanging glacier can be seen on the north face of the Breithorn.

Longitudinal crevasses (left) on the Glacier Noire (Dauphiné). Transverse crevasses and an icefall are to be seen to the right of the picture.

In the icefall of the Glacier du Géant (Mont Blanc range). The jumbled mass of ice blocks constitutes great potential hazards.

Typical marginal crevasses on the Mer de Glace (Mont Blanc chain). The glacier surface is bare and is therefore relatively free from danger.

Additional surface phenomena

One of the phenomena of a glacier is the glacier door, shown here on the Hintereis Glacier.

Apart from the opening at the end of the snout from which emerges the melt-water from the glacier, there are a number of other features to be seen on the glacier surface.

Glacier streams and glacier mills (moulins)

Melting processes produce daily a large amount of water which percolates down through the névé and flows in gullies along the surface of the ice, finally disappearing into splits in the ice.

These erosion gullies must be treated with respect as they can acquire the dimensions of normal crevasses.

Deep water holes are created by the run-off of the surface water and often grow to small lakes, the surfaces of which at low temperatures are often covered with a thin coating of ice. These holes are usually deep and their edges very smooth. Care is necessary during hours of darkness or if the ground is covered with snow.

Glacier swamps

If a glacier runs level for some distance, less thaw water flows off the surface than is formed during the day. This thaw water collects in troughs, softening up the snow and causing it to float on the top, thus creating glacier swamps.

If this freezes during the night, it can usually be walked over early next morning. As the day heats up, however, it melts again so that the swamp must be circumvented.

As it is difficult to distinguish the surface of a swamp from its background, glacier troughs must be approached with care. Although the worst that would be likely to occur if one fell in would be a thorough soaking and the abandonment of the tour, cases of drowning have been known in exceptionally deep swamps.

Glacier tables

These are large, isolated, slab-like rocks which, owing to the melting-away of the ice edges beneath, are left reposing on an ice support. As the ablation is naturally at its most effective on the south or southwest sides, there is always the danger that the table might tip over in that direction and even slide off its ice base. For this reason it is advisable to give them a wide berth.

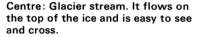

A glacier table. Dangerous in its immediate vicinity.

Centre: Glacier stream. It flows on the top of the ice and is easy to see and cross.

Above: Glacier lake. Usually deep with very smooth sides.

Dangerous snow 'balcony' over the edge of a glacier stream. It is liable to collapse at a touch.

79

Crossing a glacier in a party. Wastl Mariner: 'By employing this method of roping-up it is possible to proceed with very short rope intervals (as short as 3 metres [about 10 feet]). It is the duty of the leader and the last man to ensure that the rope is always slightly taut.'

Crevasse with a collapsed cornice bridge. A secondary bridge (below) formed of piled-up snow.

Recognition of crevasse hazards

On bare glaciers, crevasses are open and exposed and, given good visibility, can easily be recognized and avoided, so that if proper attention is paid there is no danger of falling in. On the other hand, crevasses on snow-covered glaciers are either filled with snow and barely visible, or bridged over.

Generally speaking, crevasse hazards are at their greatest in the summer after a prolonged snowfall, also in early winter when wide gaping crevasses on a bare glacier are treacherously concealed and the bridges are unsafe.

In late winter and spring the danger is less significant, for at this time the bridges have attained their greatest strength and thickness and do not soften up during the daytime.

If it is not possible to confirm the position of crevasses, experience will help us to determine where they may be expected. Hazards of crevasses can be recognized by the following distinguishing features:

1. Slight sinking or sagging of the snow cover.
2. Variations in colour of the snow, i.e. a narrow dark line.
3. Lines of rupture on the surface.
4. In summer the compact glacier is usually composed of dirty or blue-green ice and the firm névé is hard and has a blue shimmer, whereas the dangerous snow forming the bridges is white and soft.

It is a false assumption that the strength of a crevasse bridge necessarily increases with the thickness of the snow. For example, if the bridge consists of hard but brittle névé, it will bear no load at all. The strength of a snow bridge invariably depends upon the composition of the

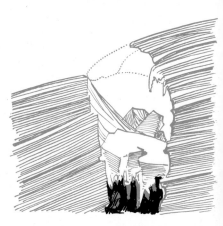

snow. In winter, especially during heavy frost, this is not reliable; in fact an accident actually occurred on the Grenz Glacier on Monte Rosa in February 1902 when, in very cold weather, a snow bridge broke under three skiers.

Opposite: This party is on the right track as they are avoiding the crevassed marginal zone of the glacier.

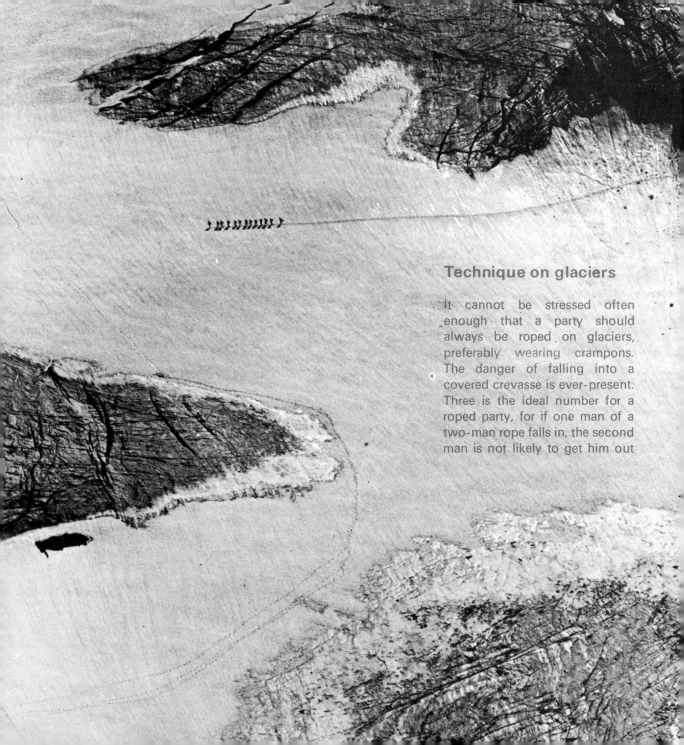

Technique on glaciers

It cannot be stressed often enough that a party should always be roped on glaciers, preferably wearing crampons. The danger of falling into a covered crevasse is ever-present. Three is the ideal number for a roped party, for if one man of a two-man rope falls in, the second man is not likely to get him out

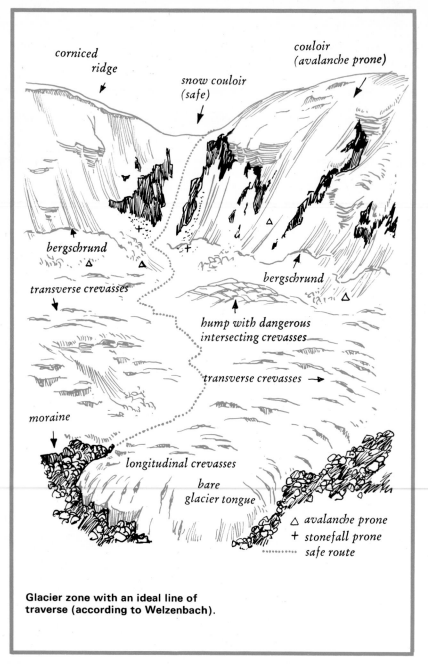

corniced ridge

couloir (avalanche prone)

snow couloir (safe)

bergschrund

bergschrund

transverse crevasses

hump with dangerous intersecting crevasses

transverse crevasses →

moraine

longitudinal crevasses

bare glacier tongue

△ *avalanche prone*
+ *stonefall prone*
⋯⋯ *safe route*

Glacier zone with an ideal line of traverse (according to Welzenbach).

alone. When roping up, a Prusik loop should be tied on in front of the knot.

As a rule, the roped party moves together, the last man keeping the rope slightly taut. Do not hold loops of rope in the hand.

While the leader pays attention to the terrain, sounds for possible crevasses with the shaft of his iceaxe and tells the second man to belay him if necessary, the other members of the party must always be prepared for the eventuality of the leader falling in. It must be made quite clear that despite the utmost care and attention it will not always be possible to check a fall while standing up: the anchor man may be pulled off his feet and be forced to check the fall lying down. This routine of checking falls should be practised beforehand, otherwise when the real emergency arises there is little real hope of holding a fall.

Choice of route on glaciers

The choice of the route to be followed must be adapted to the exigencies of the terrain. There is little fear of meeting with crevasses in glacier troughs or hollows but glacier swamps may be encountered. The track should go round humps or protuberances. If a crevasse cannot be avoided, then approach and cross it at right-angles to its length.

Ascending the Forno Glacier (Bregaglia). The track is well sited as it avoids the crevassed area.

Snow-covered glacier. The crevasses in the background are visible as they are filled with snow, whereas the surface of the glacier is bare.

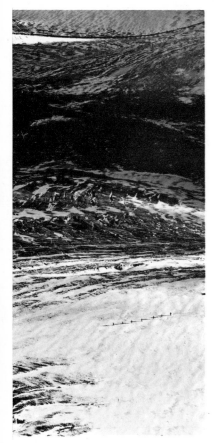

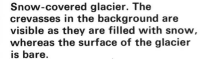

Crossing a glacier in a zone of transverse crevasses. Route lies between crevasses. Cross crevasses at right-angles.

Bergschrund on the north face of the Ötztaler Wildspitze. Even on an apparently inoffensive ordinary route such as this, the party should always be roped.

In bad visibility accurate maps to a scale of 1 : 25 000, compass and altimeter should be carried. When crossing from one side of a glacier to the other, the route should run parallel to the general line of the transverse crevasses.

If the glacier is snow-covered, a zigzag course should be kept so that the crevasses are crossed as nearly as possible at right-angles, thus preventing the arrival of a whole party together on a bridge which might conceivably collapse under the combined weight.

Crossing crevasses

Careful belaying should precede any crossing of a crevasse bridge. No more than one man should ever cross at a time. The leader should sound the bridge by slowly pushing the shaft of the iceaxe into the snow to ascertain whether the underlayer is firm enough to bear weight.

When crossing a bridge, the foot

Sounding with the iceaxe in the crevassed zone of a snow-covered glacier. The second on the rope should always belay.

Practice rescue from a crevasse.
The necessary technique should be
mastered before setting out on an
expedition.

crevasse is narrow, by reaching out to the side.

Never let go of the iceaxe in falling as it may be of immense value later on. In the case of a narrow crevasse, jamming the legs and arms against the sides, as in a chimney, may prevent any further descent.

As soon as 'firm ground' is reached a stance must be established or a further fall stopped by belaying tactics. Every party should carry at least one ice piton for this purpose.

If the fallen man is hanging uninjured and free on the rope, the technique to be adopted by the party should be the same as on rock. This technique, as has been stated time and again, should be thoroughly acquired before starting off on a climb.

should slide over the surface rather than be pressed down. If the bridge appears to be in a dangerous condition, it is better to creep over so as to distribute the weight of the body over as large a surface as possible. This surface can be increased by laying the iceaxe flat on the snow. The bridge can easily be penetrated by stepping on it, resulting in the collapse of the entire structure.

Behaviour on and after falling into a crevasse

As with a fall on rock, the climber should be mentally prepared beforehand as to his procedure rather than waiting until he finds himself at the bottom of a crevasse. If a bridge breaks, the climber can save himself from falling in by throwing his body forward and stretching out his arms in the direction of the far side of the crevasse or, if the

Fall of ice from the Ötztaler
Wildspitze. An impressive example
of the objective hazards
encountered in icefalls.

There are, generally speaking, two types of ice avalanches — firn ice and glacier ice avalanches.

Firn ice avalanches

These occur in névé regions of the upper glacier zones by the breaking-away of advancing masses of névé or the collapse of firn cornices; the avalanche quickly breaks up into a mass of moving lumps which often carry along with them accumulated snow lying in the track of the avalanche.

Flanks covered with firn snow can be very dangerous if the accumulated layers of snow become soft. Mostly they remain solid if the temperature is low and no disturbing influence intervenes. If, however, the equilibrium is disturbed, especially across the slope, the whole mass descends as an avalanche.

Glacier ice avalanches

These take place on the steeper portions of a glacier (icefall) or at fractures on steep ice walls (hanging glaciers). In the Alps large-scale icefalls and hanging glaciers are encountered principally in the western areas; in the eastern Alps they are limited to only a few places.

Ice avalanches are notoriously treacherous as they can fall at any time of the year and the very complicated relationship of tensile and pressure stresses present

in an icefall or a hanging glacier is far beyond any reliable computation.

A rise in temperature either by day or night increases the danger, although the thunder of ice avalanches can often be heard on frosty winter nights.

As soon as the equilibrium of a sérac or a hanging glacier is disturbed, it will fall; in fact a sérac may be brought to fall by the wind.

An example of this is afforded by the celebrated 'Swiss Roll' (Schaumrolle) above the north face of the Königsspitze. For decades it had menaced the Ertl route and was even scaled by Kurt Diemberger, until it finally collapsed in 1962. It is true that a wide crack had been observed at the top, but who goes to the top of a mountain before starting the climb to see if the cornice is safe or not?

Protection against ice avalanches

The only way to dodge ice avalanches is to avoid faces containing hanging glaciers or to make a detour around icefalls. The front or downstream side of séracs is particularly dangerous. The foot of a wall in the fall line of a hanging glacier is usually covered with ice blocks and debris. The external appearance of these blocks gives an indica- of the time of the last fall. If the debris has sharp edges, the fall is of recent date; on the other hand, blocks melted by the sun suggest an older avalanche.

Ice avalanches often fall at more or less stated intervals, so that after long observation a relatively reliable time-scale can be established.

Behaviour in ice avalanches

Every climber must realize that the destructive power of an ice avalanche is far greater than one of snow.

During the summer of 1965, the Allalin Glacier in the Valaisan Alps was the scene of a catastrophe. An ice avalanche fell from its snout during the night into the Saas Valley killing eighty-eight dam workers in their huts. The last body was not dug out of the debris until August 1967. Even small ice avalanches are extremely dangerous on account of the extensive area of devastation. A cubic metre (about 35 cubic feet) of ice weighs nearly 2000 pounds so that even a small avalanche can amount to many tons.

Emergency precautions: Ram in the iceaxe, arms on top with head well down and body as close to the wall as possible. Jump into a crevasse if available, as this is preferable to exposure to an ice avalanche. The French guide, Lionel Terray, once did this when a large sérac fell on the Freney Glacier in the Mont Blanc range, thereby saving his life. His client's reaction was not so quick — and he died.

The rope should be checked for damage after ice or stonefall.

Ice walls

This is not the place to enter into the technique of climbing on ice, as there are plenty of technical books on the subject. Moreover, neither rock nor ice climbing can be learned from textbooks; practice, more practice and long years of experience are necessary.

The texture of the ice has a direct relationship with ice technique. As distinct from objective dangers such as avalanches, falling ice and cornices and weather conditions, one has also to reckon with subjective hazards.

Inexperienced climbers frequently catch the front points of the crampons in the stockings, especially when moving the inside foot forwards.

If the second man is in the direct fall line of the leader, he is liable to be showered with ice particles if the latter is too vigorous with his step-cutting. Care should be exercised in cutting steps on

verglas, as parts of the surface are liable to come away if the ice coating is adhering to the underlying rock. Any loose particles must be removed before driving in a piton. Attention must be paid to snow balling up on the crampons which will consequently impede safe climbing. There are now crampons on the market made of an alloy which largely prevents adherence of snow.

Hard winter ice on the great ice slope of the north face of the Matterhorn. Nicky Clough and her husband Ian, who was killed on Annapurna in May 1970.

Behaviour in case of a fall

This technique should be practised beforehand on a convenient ice slope. If the fall occurs on sloping ground, keep hold of the iceaxe and make the body as stiff as possible in order to achieve the maximum possible friction on the slope. Do not bring the points of the crampons in contact with the slope as they are likely to cause the falling man to overbalance and continue the descent head-foremost. It is just possible to check a fall by pressing in the pick of the iceaxe level with the chest (one hand grasps the pick and the other holds the shaft). The pick should be pressed in fairly gently, otherwise the axe could be torn from the hands.

Ice screws are the best adjuncts for belaying on an ice slope (long screws for unsound ice and

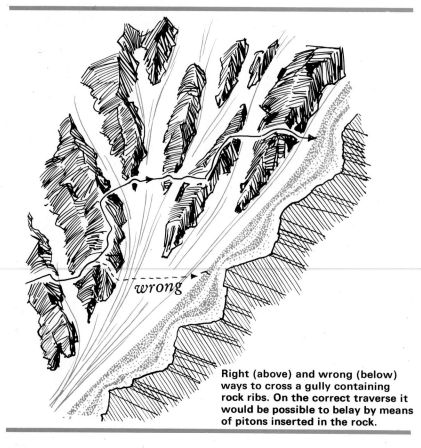

Right (above) and wrong (below) ways to cross a gully containing rock ribs. On the correct traverse it would be possible to belay by means of pitons inserted in the rock.

wrong

shorter ones for hard ice). A few rock pitons should also be carried in case a rock outcrop is encountered.

Ice gullies

These form the natural track for falling stones and ice, unstable cornices and avalanches. Moral: Never ascend an ice gully. Suppose, however, that it is impossible to avoid an ascent or, like the celebrated Pallavicini Couloir on the Gross Glockner, it relates to a well-known and spectacular ice climb. In that case, start the climb early and do not ascend in the bed of the couloir as there the danger of avalanches, stone and icefall is at its maximum. There are also good opportunities for belaying at the edges if the rock is sound enough to take a piton.

If no ice screw is available, it may be possible to ram in the pick of the iceaxe and form a belay with a well dug-in rope loop; this is, however, not very secure.

Grooves in the snow caused by falling stones at the foot of walls and gullies. Formation of a so-called 'secondary ice gully'.

Mountain weather

Given good weather and satisfactory conditions, the average mountaineer can undertake difficult expeditions with safety. Mountaineering skill and bodily and spiritual qualities are first put to the test at the approach of unsatisfactory conditions, i.e. sudden change in the weather, storm and cold, sudden icing-up of the rocks or an unexpected fall of snow in difficult terrain. Only then will mature experience prove its worth.

The climber should invariably have a little in reserve so that in case of difficulties arising he can pull something out of the bag.

A thunderstorm in the making. 'Cauliflower' clouds ascend from the valley. The cloud formation in the foreground is not conducive to precipitation. The top part of the clouds in the background, however, which resemble cottonwool, have already reached the ice—snow stage and presage the outbreak of rain and thunderstorms.

Before the storm.

Meteorological conditions in the Alps

No accurate determination of weather conditions throughout the year in alpine territory can be given as the weather on the north side of the alpine chain is less reliable than on the south; and alpine weather is very changeable. The following data may be taken as an average and, in the main, can be considered as dependable.

January
Reasonably dry. Frequent high atmospheric pressure brings cold weather mainly to the valleys which often lie under cloud cover. Above this, the sun shines and high temperatures prevail.

February
More precipitation. Frequent snowfalls, which set and last until well into the summer.

March
Wet. Still snowfalls in the heights. First föhn storms, causing wet snow avalanches (grundlawinen).

April
Wet. Very unreliable with frequent föhn storms.

May
Cold spell about the middle of the month. Frequent snowfalls right down into the valleys.

June
Again a cold spell towards the middle of the month, lasting a little longer, accompanied by showers of rain and giving rise to the first severe summer thunderstorms.

July
Often a wet month.

August
Weather much more reliable and remains comparatively good for the first three weeks. During the last week there is a tendency to storms and snowfall in the high Alps.

September
Commencement of autumn in the high regions. The weather is generally fine, lasting throughout the month. Excellent visibility but distinctly cold nights.

October
Continuation of the September weather. Much colder at night. Last month of summer mountaineering.

November
Mist, snowfalls and föhn storms in the upper regions.

December
Continuation of November weather up to the first snowfalls, shortly before, during or shortly after Christmas. Increasing cold and higher atmospheric pressure.

94

Weather signs

Very high, rapidly moving and more-or-less fleecy clouds (cirrus) usually bring bad weather within the next eight to fifteen hours.

If cirro-cumulus clouds travel very rapidly from southwest to west in a milky sky, showers are to be expected.

Lowering and broken-up cloud covering the sky indicates rain or snow within the next twenty minutes or so.

If a light breeze blows up the mountain in the morning and at night, and down towards the valley during the day, the weather will deteriorate before long.

The sudden appearance of a high-level airstream denotes the approach of a low-pressure area.

Föhn is nearly always followed by a fall in temperature, often accompanied by a fall of new snow.

cirrus clouds

cirro-cumulus clouds

strato-cumulus clouds

Cloud forms

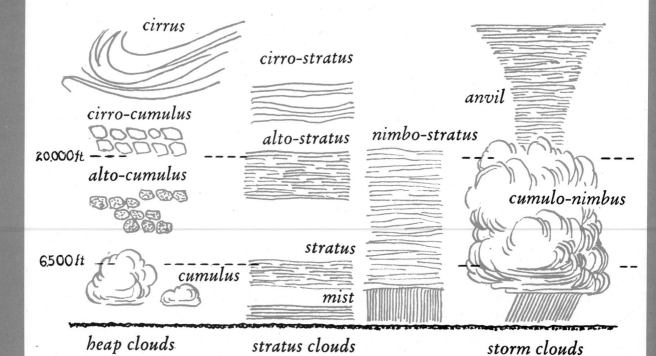

cirrus

cirro-stratus

cirro-cumulus

anvil

20,000 ft

alto-stratus

nimbo-stratus

alto-cumulus

cumulo-nimbus

stratus

6,500 ft

cumulus

mist

heap clouds

stratus clouds

storm clouds

Weather forecasting with the altimeter

the Bézard compass

both indispensable

a modern altimeter

An altimeter is a pocket barometer with air-pressure and height scales. It is based on the fact that barometric pressure decreases with increasing height.

The external circle is graduated, probably in 10- or 20-metre intervals. The local air pressure, as well as that at sea level, can be read off the inner, stationary circle in millimetres.

Given a constant height (e.g. in the hut at night or in the valley) the altimeter can be used as a barometer for forecasting purposes. There is much that can upset a weather forecast – clouds, for example – but at least an altimeter will give an accurate forecast for the next twelve to twenty-four hours.

The following twelve Rules for Barometers drawn up by the Swiss Alpine Club should be memorized by every owner of an altimeter.

1. If the pressure rises appreciably (4–6 mm) in the course of a few hours, the fine weather will be only of short duration.

2. If the pressure rises rapidly during the course of the day, fine weather can be expected, the duration of which depends upon the amount of rise. If the rise lasts only one day, the fine weather will not last much longer.

3. If the pressure rises slowly, uniformly and steadily for two or more days, a long spell of dry weather is in sight. If, at the same time, the wind goes round from the west to the north, the weather will shortly clear up.

4. If the wind veers from south to west and north, accompanied by a pronounced rise in pressure, better weather will ensue.

5. If the pressure attains an unusually high level with moist atmosphere and in calm conditions, fog or mist can be expected, followed as a rule by good weather.

6. If the pressure rises rapidly by fits and starts, interspersed by slight falls, unsettled weather will follow. The same applies in the case of rapid and spasmodic falling, interrupted by short rises.

7. Falling pressure points to rain if, at the same time, the wind veers from north or east to south or southwest.

8. Long and continuous falling indicates a long and continuous period of rain; the longer the fall the longer the rainy period. If the barometer falls rapidly to a very low level, a downpour accompanied by strong wind is imminent.

9. A thunderstorm is to be expected if the pressure falls rapidly, but not too low, in calm and warm conditions, particularly in summer with increasing humidity of the atmosphere.

10. If the fall continues between 10.30 and 11.30 am, rain will unquestionably set in before long. If the wind is in the west the rain will come within twenty-four hours, a little later with an easterly wind.

11. If the pressure rises only in the afternoon, fine weather will follow but will not last for long.

12. If the pressure falls only during the afternoon, this is of little importance, especially in summer.

Apart from following these rules of forecasting, the hut guardian should be asked about the weather before setting out. Nearly every mountain area has its own weather signs which can be satisfactorily interpreted only by the hut guardian or other locals.

Wind and cold

Wind and cold cannot be set apart from mountain hazards. Wind increases evaporation from those parts of the body exposed to the air and rapidly brings about supercooling. If there is no wind, cold alone can be endured to a much higher degree.

High wind

The strength of the wind increases with the height. Very high winds are as a rule encountered only in the central eastern and western Alps, and often in clear weather and extreme cold. Many a climber has had to abandon an ascent just before the summit on account of violent wind. Sudden gusts can easily throw a man to the ground, blow him off an exposed ridge or hurl him to one side

Thunderstorm on the Langen Ferner Glacier in the Ortler range.

when abseiling.

The strength and direction of the wind can usually be recognized from the valley by the movement of the clouds and the existence of snow plumes on summits and ridges.

Bottom right: Winter storm on the Grubigstein in the Lechtaler Alps.

Wind force

Every mountaineer should know the wind-force scale which forms the basis of official weather reports and the features on most weather charts. This is furnished by the Beaufort Scale, devised by the French Admiral Beaufort in 1800 and which serves as a basis on land and sea for the determination of wind force.

Cold

As the force of the wind increases on the tops, so does the temperature fall, at a rate of about 0·5 to 1 °C per 100 metres. For example, the temperature on the summit of the Zugspitze is about 10 to 12 °C lower than in Garmisch-Partenkirchen, and on Mont Blanc about 37 °C lower than in Chamonix. It is thus possible to calculate in the valley or at the hut at what altitude the snow

Beaufort scale of wind force

			Speed (miles per hour)
0	Calm	Smoke rises vertically	Less than 1
1	Light air	Smoke drifts	1–3
2	Light breeze	Wind felt on face, leaves rustle	4–7
3	Gentle breeze	Leaves and small twigs in constant motion	8–12
4	Moderate breeze	Small branches are moved	13–18
5	Fresh breeze	Small trees in leaf begin to sway. Unpleasant	19–24
6	Strong breeze	Large branches in motion. Umbrellas used with difficulty	25–31
7	Moderate gale	Whole trees in motion	32–38
8	Fresh gale	Generally impedes progress	39–46
9	Strong gale	Slates and tiles removed	47–54
10	Whole gale	Trees uprooted	55–63
11	Storm	Widespread damage	64–75
12	Hurricane	General devastation	Above 75

is likely to be encountered. Although a fine balance is maintained between the giving-off of heat by the body and production of heat by it, this so-called 'thermodynamic freedom' can be placed in jeopardy by the action of external cold. Wind and moisture are the greatest dangers, for much more heat is given off by the body through the evaporation effect of wet clothing than is the case with very low temperatures under dry conditions.

Extreme cold reduces the bodily efficiency and the psychological resistance to their lowest degree; it can cause men to become completely listless and apathetic.*

Defensive measures (warm and windproof clothing, high food intake) against the effect of cold must be adopted in good time, otherwise it may be too late.

Certain parts of the body are particularly susceptible to frost-bite, such as fingers, toes, nose and ears. The fingers are usually the first to feel the effect. If they are unprotected by gloves they lose the sense of touch so that it is difficult to grasp holds or use the iceaxe. They can usually be restored by putting them in your pockets or against a warm part of the body; this causes a tingling sensation, a sign that they are thawing out.

The toes are particularly liable to frostbite if the boots are tight. Although nowadays there are climbing boots specially designed to prevent freezing, the danger still exists. Badly fitting boots, overtightening of the crampon straps, etc. can restrict the circulation and bring about frostbite which is often not discovered until it is too late. To mitigate this, wriggle your toes to maintain blood circulation in your feet; and avoid overtight lacing etc.

* In Britain, the danger from 'exposure' which can lead to 'hypothermia' has been identified as a major mountain hazard in bad weather, especially among young people and those with inadequate clothing. The British Mountaineering Council (see footnote on page 131) has issued a leaflet, 'Exposure', on the dangers and treatment.

Storm high up on the Grand Combin (Canton Valais).

Protection against wind and cold

The body is generally kept sufficiently warm when moving, but when resting, belaying or in a bivouac, it soon cools off. The first sign of this is a chilly feeling which increases until the body is shivering. If the cooling-off process increases, these convulsive muscular movements cease and unconsciousness supervenes.

Three basic principles against wind and cold:
1. Warm, dry clothing.
2. Movement.
3. Suitable food.

To be a complete protection, however, these points should not be considered separately but adopted as a composite whole.

Clothing

The importance of clothing for the mountaineer is often underestimated. It can nevertheless increase or reduce his efficiency under conditions of heat or cold. The most important tasks of clothing are the regulation of the temperature changes in the body, the carrying-off of sweat,

the retaining of bodily heat and of ventilation. The retaining of bodily heat means the amount of air that can be retained in close proximity to the body by the clothing and kept there despite the external movement of air.

The process of the carrying-off of sweat can present a problem with perlon and nylon as they are not very satisfactory for this purpose. A moist tropical 'microclimate' is formed between the

clothing and the skin, with all its unpleasant consequences. Good ventilation is therefore necessary, especially when walking uphill, but the clothing should be capable of being closed up for cooler conditions also. In particular sleeves and the knee-fastenings of breeches should be capable of being easily buttoned up; the same applies to the collar. In this manner, violent sweating can be avoided on the

The photographer called this 'Young couple in a snowstorm'! It does, however, emphasize the protection of a bivouac sack in sudden changes in the weather.

ascent and when cold the flow of air can be retarded, resulting in maintenance of warmth.

Practical clothing is always to be preferred to fashionable dress. What is the use of beautiful finger gloves if the fingers freeze up more easily than in wool mittens?

Movement

Movement during an expedition is generally a *sine qua non*. The exceptions are on very difficult rock or ice climbs when one may have to stay more or less motionless for hours belaying on a small stance. A climber in such a position must at all costs attempt to keep warm but not, of course, at the expense of neglecting belaying tactics.

As a rule, it will be possible only to beat the arms against the body and gently move the legs. This is a much more difficult operation if one is standing in slings, as hardly any movement is possible. Another hazard here is the cutting action of the harness into the body which can soon result in freezing. Once again, circulatory promotion tablets work wonders.

Food

After clothing, suitable food is of supreme importance in keeping out the cold. Franz Nieberl and Toni Hiebeler in *Das Klettern im Fels* ['Rock Climbing'] have the following to say on this subject:

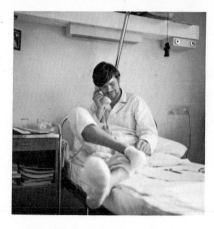

Reinhold Messner back from Nanga Parbat with severe frostbite (six toes amputated), in Innsbruck University Clinic. After his descent he dragged himself along the ground for several days without food.

One is more and more forced to the conclusion not only that solid food and meat can be dispensed with but also that vegetable products, and liquid nourishment in particular, lead to much greater and lasting bodily efficiency. The ingestion of solid foods containing fat and albumen products should be avoided as far as possible. Fatty substances necessitate a long and often unsettling digestive process. Albumen involves the consumption of a great deal of oxygen, which is precisely what is lacking at high altitudes. Quite apart from the bodily exertion which is neither permitted nor overcome by an overloading of the digestive organs, the customary foods (meat, sausage, butter, pastry, etc.) are no longer palatable in very cold conditions. The weight and volume of the

conventional types of food can amount to as much as 3 to 4 kg [2–4½ lb] for a three-day tour, whereas one can get away with about 500 to 800 gm [1–1¾ lb] with modern foodstuffs. These include such articles as 'Sanddorn' fruit juice (sanddorn is a spiky plant growing on the sea shore), whole corn rusks and vegetable broth. This latter is important on account of its salt content, as bodily exertion involves a considerable loss of salt. 100 gm [3½ oz] of 'sanddorn' berries contain 600 mg% of Vitamin C (blackcurrants contain 180 mg%, lemons 80 mg%). The daily Vitamin C intake for men in a normal job should amount to 75 mg.

Mist and drifting snow

Mist and drifting snow or blizzards which limit the visibility test the mountaineer to an exceptional degree and greatly increase the difficulty of an ascent. They occur so often that they must always be taken into consideration.

An expedition, which in fine weather can be regarded as child's play, can present the climber with a difficult problem if mist or drifting snow are present.

How and where mist occurs
If moist air lying close to the ground cools off, local or widespread ground mist will occur. A typical case is where a blanket of mist overlies valleys and plains, often for a day or more, above which the sun is shining.

Another development similar to ground mist in its effect occurs higher up and is due to cloud layers which conceal the summits and spread down the flanks sometimes as far as the valley. This type of mist can be extremely dangerous for the climber as it can change its position very rapidly, suddenly enveloping him and making orientation extremely difficult.

Ascent to the Panossière hut in mist. The climber is tested to an exceptional degree.

Hazards of mist and driving snow

On névé and ice
When mist and drifting snow set in everything assumes a strange, unearthly form and distances are very difficult to estimate. Rocks, actually only a few feet away, appear remote, pinnacles and ribs disappear and walls and faces take on a steeper and un-symmetrical aspect.

On the level white areas of snowy plateaux and on slopes and glaciers no landmarks are visible and orientation becomes virtually impossible. The line of demarcation between mist and ground can often not be determined by the eye; in the vague light it is not possible to tell whether one is going up or down and frequently the groping foot is required to assume the task which the eye can no longer perform.

The danger of getting lost is especially prevalent in the intricacies of an icefall. The disheartening effect which an adventure of this nature could have upon an inexperienced mountaineer is quite enough to reduce his efficiency just at the moment when all his mental faculties should be at their maximum pitch.

The visibility in mist varies to a remarkable degree. The average range of sight in mist of from 50 to 100 yards can be reduced to a few feet, particularly if it is snowing as well. Even with a slight mist and a little snow it is quite possible not to see a nearby chasm or to approach too near the edge of a cornice.

On rock
In limestone or dolomite mountains which are of terraced formation and have a number of debris-covered ledges, it is often

Valley or ground mist constitutes no hazard for the climber higher up.

extremely difficult with low visibility to determine which is the right ledge to use for the ascent or descent. These mountains in general require a much higher sense of orientation than is the case with more straightforward terrain if the visibility is low.

Route-finding on high plateaux is very difficult when visibility is poor if there is a complete lack of landmarks.

The formation of walls and ridges in most gneiss mountains is of classical simplicity when compared to the jumble of cracks, gullies, couloirs, towers and pinnacles which form part of limestone and dolomite mountains. As Paulcke remarked, the route of ascent is arbitrarily dictated in the granite mountains. That does not mean to infer that high qualities of route-finding are not necessary in the gneiss and granite ranges.

Apart from the difficulty of route-finding in mist there is always the ever-present danger of precipitation. Damp fog or drizzle can wet the rock face and, if it is cold as well, can cover the surface with a thin coating of ice. This glazing (verglas) increases the difficulty of the climb.

Surfaces covered with grass or vegetation are also subject to this glazing, making them extremely hazardous.

Opposite: There is no difficulty in route-finding on the first few pitches of the Yellow Rib on the Kleine Zinne; 80 metres higher up, however, where the rib is less well defined on the wide face, mist could add to the problem of orientation.

Behaviour in mist and driving snow

On névé and ice

As soon as the threat of mist or driving snow becomes apparent, the exact position on the map must be determined, which must then be used for route-finding. Every mountaineer should be familiar with the use of map, compass and altimeter. When descending, the skier should go slowly as speed is deceptive and it is not always possible to pinpoint the landmarks.

In icefalls it is advisable to mark the route (by tracking marks or using red marking flags) so that in the event of a retreat it will be possible to retrace one's steps. Always keep together, even though separation for the purpose of route-finding appears attractive. Tracks (especially ski tracks) covered by new or drift snow can usually be felt under foot. Old foot and ski tracks occasionally stand out on the surface and may remain in that state for months. If orientation has become impossible it is useless and dangerous to go on. If possible, it is best to return to the last known landmark and try to start again, assuming of course that bodily fitness permits. In case of doubt a bivouac with suitable equipment (which every mountaineer should have) is infinitely preferable and less hazardous than blindly wandering about and trusting to luck to find a way out.

On rock

The conditions prevailing on rock are, up to a point, the same as on snow or ice when the mist comes down. It is important to observe any peculiarities of the terrain, such as outstanding and prominent rock formations and any

Soon there will be rain and snow on the Mont Blanc range.

variations in colour of the rock or ice. On the ascent keep looking about and take note of details such as abseil stances and variations in route for the descent. No pitch looks the same from above as it does from below.

Small cairns should also be erected or red marking flags laid out (weighed down with a stone), especially where there is a change in direction.

Leave footprints in the snow on snow-covered ledges, even if it means going out of the way to do so. In rocky terrain it is often possible to determine one's position by the branching off of lateral ridges or sharp bends in the main ridge if the climber has previously made himself familiar with the form and structure of the mountain.

Not too much reliance should be placed on guide books, as I have found to my own cost. For this reason, in low visibility an ascent should not be attempted which has no outstanding characteristics such as well-defined ridges, chimneys, gullies, etc.

Paulcke: 'A climber must learn to know the terrain like a work of art, assimilate it and comprehend it like a scientific publication. The more perfectly he is able to do so, the better will he understand the terrain in the same way as an artist dominates his instrument and the scholar his profession.'

thick stratus clouds

rain clouds

storm clouds

Thunderstorms and rain

Local thunderstorms, the so-called 'heat storms', occur very frequently in the summer. Long periods of fine weather accompanied by the equal distribution of a high-pressure system all over Europe are the most favourable conditions for local thunderstorms.

These storms are preceded by calm weather. According to the situation of the valleys, the air masses above them heat up to varying degrees until the disturbance of the equilibrium of their varying temperatures eventually causes thunderstorms. Thus, they take place after the sun has reached its zenith and are emphatically an afternoon occurrence.

How to recognize the advent of thunderstorms

There exist quite a few signs with which every mountaineer should be acquainted: formation of massive cumulus clouds above the mountain crests at midday; quiet calm air combined with great heat, i.e. oppressive, sultry atmosphere with a cloudless morning sky.

Cumulo-nimbus clouds, which usually make their appearance early in the morning very high in the sky (2000–3000 metres), produce prominent light-coloured towers arising above the flat cloud layer. Shortly before the storm breaks, these cumulus clouds grow to majestic proportions ('storm towers' or 'turrets'). The distance of a thunderstorm can be determined by experiment: divide the time in seconds between the lightning and the thunder by five. From this can be calculated the distance in miles, five seconds being equal to one mile. Thunder can usually be heard over a distance of between 6 and 16 miles, depending upon the height of any intervening elevations.

Behaviour in thunderstorms

Apart from the danger of lightning, which is dealt with separately, there still remains rain which occurs either during or after the storm. This does not hold any significance for the mountaineer, compared with other hazards, as long as he can keep on the move. If progress is impossible or only after a long enforced halt, the clothing can become wet enough to produce supercooling of the body which can be very dangerous.

If the storm is seen to be purely local, the best thing to do is to shelter under the bivouac sack, after taking all necessary precautions against lightning, and await the end of the storm. Do not take up a position in gullies or chimneys as they can readily become channels for watercourses or falling stones.

The rope should be protected from the rain, for even the latest perlon ropes absorb water; they thus become heavier and run with difficulty through the karabiners.

Particular care should be exercised when abseiling in or after rain. Wet clothing and ropes do not permit a steady and uniform descent but only by fits and starts, which brings about a dangerous back-pull on the abseil piton.

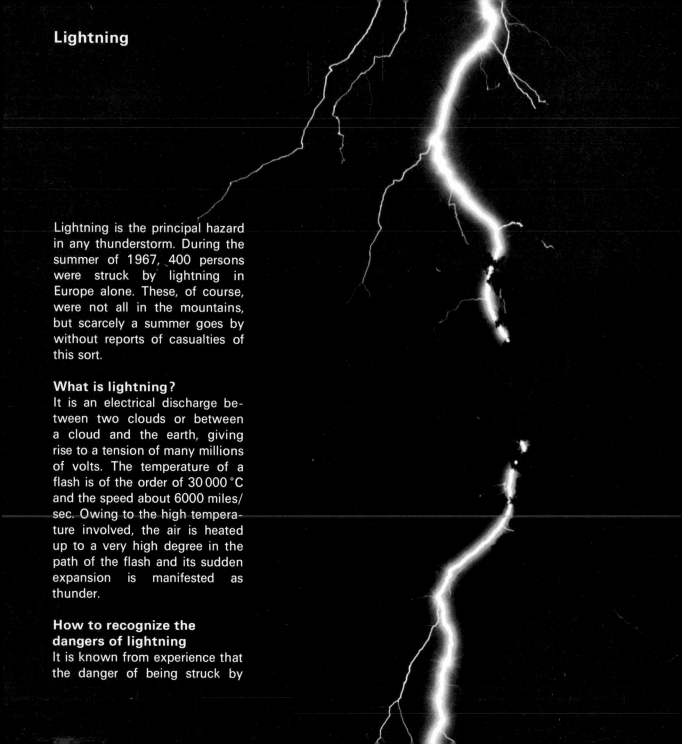

Lightning

Lightning is the principal hazard
in any thunderstorm. During the
summer of 1967, 400 persons
were struck by lightning in
Europe alone. These, of course,
were not all in the mountains,
but scarcely a summer goes by
without reports of casualties of
this sort.

What is lightning?
It is an electrical discharge between two clouds or between
a cloud and the earth, giving
rise to a tension of many millions
of volts. The temperature of a
flash is of the order of 30 000 °C
and the speed about 6000 miles/
sec. Owing to the high temperature involved, the air is heated
up to a very high degree in the
path of the flash and its sudden
expansion is manifested as
thunder.

How to recognize the
dangers of lightning
It is known from experience that
the danger of being struck by

Relatively safe (×) and dangerous (arrowed) zones when lightning is about.

lightning is greater on rock than on snow or ice. The presence of electrical discharge generally makes itself felt as follows:

1. Unprotected parts of the skin feel as though they were touched by a spider's web.
2. Tickling of the scalp.
3. Standing-up of the hair.
4. 'Singing' of metal objects.
5. A slight crackling and the appearance of a blue light (St Elmo's Fire) on prominent metal objects, such as summit crosses etc.

These are all signs of a static discharge, the so-called static electricity within the area of the storm. If this static discharge is not compensated by the voltage tension, lightning will strike.

There are, however, other exceptions: if a neutral cloud, having no influence upon the earth, is situated below the thundercloud, both clouds constitute a condenser. If the discharge takes place between these two clouds, the tension between the lowest cloud and the earth increases suddenly to such a degree that a discharge takes place towards the earth. In such a case there is no previous warning on the ground.

On summits which are frequently struck by lightning (e.g. the Tribulaun) cairns are destroyed

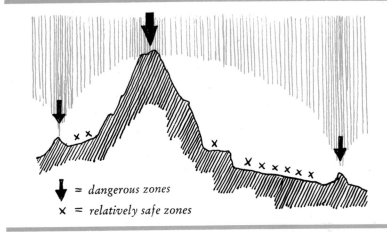

↓ = *dangerous zones*

× = *relatively safe zones*

Strong earth currents (in direction of arrows) emanating from lightning higher up. If possible do not take shelter in chimneys or under overhangs.

The space hatched in blue is safe from a direct hit by lightning.

Fixed cables and iron stanchions such as these should be avoided if lightning is about. In any case, take care that they are not loose or damaged.

Strong earth currents in direction of arrows. The man to the right is in danger. The man to the left with drawn-up legs is in a safe position.

Earth currents (arrowed) can jump over hollows. This man is in danger.

and very often the rock is covered with 'lightning glaze' (Blitzverglasung) up to a millimetre in depth. The enormous heat generated by the lightning melts the rock surface and vitrifies it.

How to combat the threat of lightning

The frequently expressed theory that lightning strikes only the highest point is only partly correct. An electrically charged cloud may be just below the summit so that the lightning discharges onto a lower secondary peak or onto the extreme end of a ridge.

How should the climber conduct himself in the presence of a threat of lightning?

1. Avoid summits and ridges or any exposed points at all costs, and do not approach them nearer than about 15 yards. The effect at a distance of 150 yards is much less than close to.

2. Metal articles of equipment should, as far as possible, be placed at some distance.

3. Gullies containing water, streams, cracks filled up with earth, cavities, recesses and their outlets (short-circuit gaps) and lone trees should be avoided.

4. Overhangs and recesses are no protection against earth currents.

5. Holding onto wire cables is very dangerous and any

It is ill-advised to take shelter under a lone boulder lying on scree during a storm. A position a few yards distant will provide almost complete safety.

route equipped with such safety measures should not be contemplated.

6. Any dry spot on which one crouches should be situated not less than 3 feet from any vertical cliff, which should also be five to ten times higher than the person taking shelter. The minimum distance from a rock pinnacle should not be less than 15 yards.

7. Take up a squatting position with knees drawn up and both feet together. This is the best protection against earth currents.

8. If one is caught out on a climb by a thunderstorm, belaying tactics must be at once adopted. Several belays are advisable as the rope could be severed by lightning.

9. When abseiling, keep the feet together and touching the wall. There is little danger

Both the man to the right and to the left are in danger-spots. Earth currents might be conducted through the crack on the right by water, and the position on the left is also dangerous.

if the rope is dry.

10. A tent standing in the open is exposed to lightning. During a storm, assume a crouching position and do not touch the walls of the tent.

11. There are some fixed bivouacs which have no earthed conductors. In such a case, lying on the bunk wrapped in blankets affords the best protection.

Ropes should always be placed at right-angles to the flow of earth currents. The belay on the left is not safe.

Behaviour during a
break in the weather

If climbers are surprised by a sudden break in the weather, lower terrain protected from the wind must be sought out at once, for this often portends the onset of a long period of bad weather lasting a week or even longer.

If caught in a bivouac one can virtually become a prisoner of the mountain, for by next morning wintry conditions most likely will have set in. Continuation of the ascent or even a descent may become impossible and one may have to rely on assistance provided by the mountain rescue services, always assuming that they have been able to receive distress signals in time.

A so-called 'popular weather maxim' is a red sky in the morning which indicates an impending break in the weather.

Southerly winds usually precede bad weather, and föhn in the northern alpine winter means the same thing.

Another certain sign is a thunderstorm in the early morning, late in the evening or during the night. This almost certainly foretells a rainy day.

If a party has started out on a tour, despite a falling barometer, a red dawn and high clouds (cirrus), they should watch out for clouds in the west or north, so that the climb can be abandoned in time.

A break in the weather accompanied by an influx of cold air always takes place earlier at lower altitudes. Massive, low-lying, cumulus-type clouds appear on the horizon with rain streaming from the lower edges to the earth. These are the so-called 'squall clouds' which are usually followed by bad weather in the summer months. If high cirrus formation occurs, a front storm is imminent which indicates the onset of a weather break followed by a long period

of bad weather. Unlike local thunderstorms, which occur in the warm season, weather breaks can take place at any time of the year. They are a concomitant phenomenon of a low-pressure area extending over a large part of the Alps (mostly in the north) associated with a big drop in temperature.

This sudden influx of cold air is accompanied by a change in wind direction, and tempestuous winds at a great height veering from west to north often last for days on end.

The föhn

föhn clouds

If a low-pressure area is approaching the Alps, air flows down from the crests and heats up during its downward passage to become a dry, warm wind. The föhn is usually at its most powerful between October and May and brings about unusually high temperatures.

How to recognize the föhn

Even the most cautious of mountaineers can quite unexpectedly get caught in a föhn stream, although it may be quite cold in the valley. Unless he has not already been put into the picture by weather-wise valley dwellers who have a 'nose' for these things, the climber should be warned of the presence of föhn by the appearance of the föhn wall, a peculiar bluish tint of the snow-covered mountains and the blackish-green colour of the forests.

Another characteristic of the föhn is the appearance of the so-called 'föhn fishes'. These are clouds in line-ahead, looking like roughly torn cottonwool; they usually have brilliantly white edges. They float along, one after another, rather like a shoal of fish. As they approach the sun they tend to become irised, that is to say they exhibit spots, bands or arcs of a predominantly rose-coloured or emerald-green hue.

A rapid appreciation of the presence of föhn is eminently necessary, for temperatures of above freezing point in the high Alps in winter can cause deterioration of the snow and lead to wet snow avalanches. When the föhn is blowing, bad weather is nearly always present on the crests and the lee sides of the mountains.

Hazards due to föhn

Although the weather in the valleys may be good during the föhn, one should not minimize the dangers it may bring in its wake.

The föhn is nearly always followed as a matter of course by a break in the weather accompanied by precipitation and a drop in temperature. Owing to the warmth associated with the föhn there is increased danger of stonefall and avalanches. The higher temperature, combined with increased moisture of the air, causes overheating and consequent bodily fatigue. There are many people who suffer from attacks of vertigo and general indisposition brought on by this wind.

Never under any circumstances start a tour if the föhn is blowing. You may well get away with it, but what does it matter if a tour has to be abandoned?

Walter Hofmeister has a word for it: 'Rather turn back ten times too early than once too late.'

113

Mountain sickness is at its worst in the so-called 'Zone of Death', over 7000 metres in the Himalayas.

This climber on the summit of Everest is protecting himself from its effects by wearing an oxygen mask.

On the summit of Chimbaya in the Andes (6010 m). The lack of oxygen in the atmosphere is very noticeable. A hat with a wide brim gives protection against solar radiation.

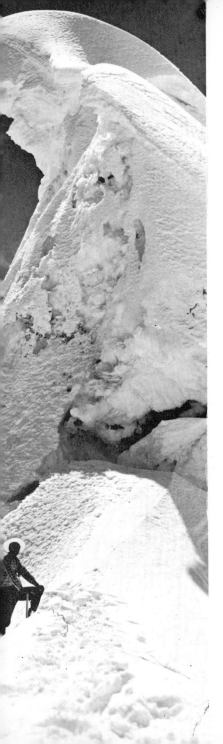

Mountain sickness and solar radiation

Efficiency on alpine tours depends upon the adaptation of the body to heights. There are mountaineers who can ascend anything at low heights but above 3000 metres become progressively weaker and over 4000 metres can do no more.

Mountain sickness

It is an interesting fact that this affects younger persons more than those of a mature age. It is well known that each cell of the human body needs oxygen. However, at high altitudes less total pressure prevails so that the gases of which the atmosphere is composed, one of the most important of which is oxygen, have less partial pressure so that there is less of this element available. Up to a height of 2000 metres the deficiency of oxygen is compensated for by the lungs. Over and above this altitude — the partial pressure of the oxygen having dropped by one-quarter — the reserves of the lungs are no longer sufficient. The marrow of the bones forms fresh red blood corpuscles which are present in the blood circulation and which transport the oxygen.

There are other factors which have a crippling effect upon the bodily well-being, such as depression, loss of self-confidence, fear, etc., apart from any climatic developments which may intervene.

Preventative measures

As we have seen in the short introduction to this section, there is only one preparatory measure for a sojourn in the heights, namely acclimatization. Although the way this is carried out varies according to the individual — extreme variations in temperature and the effect of solar radiation increase the onset of mountain sickness — there are a few basic rules for the prevention of this malady.

1. Before undertaking tours at very great altitudes, ascend lower summits or remain at the hut in order to get accustomed to the lack of oxygen.
2. Plenty of sleep is necessary before starting out. Drink only small amounts of alcohol.
3. Anyone not feeling at the top of his form should refrain from undertaking a tour at great heights.
4. Have plenty of protection against cold and heat.
5. Do not rush, climb slowly.
6. Do not make breathing difficult by too narrow a harness or too heavy a rucksack. A full stomach and bowels also affect the respiration. Eat sparingly but do not climb on an empty stomach.
7. It is much better to eat less more often.
8. Breathe slowly and talk as little as possible.
9. Smoke little or not at all.

As regards a protracted stay in regions higher than the Alps, scientific investigation has shown that full acclimatization without using oxygen is possible only at heights of up to 5500 metres. The Englishman Frank Smythe, however, reached an altitude of 8572 metres on Everest on 1 June 1933 without having to resort to the use of oxygen.

Forms of mountain sickness

These usually appear at about 4000 metres. If, however, the ascent has been made by mountain railway it may already be too late.

The brain is the part most susceptible to the lack of oxygen, causing fatigue, inertia and lack of willpower. This is followed by a feeling of vertigo, nausea and vomiting. If bleeding from the mucous membranes occurs, then the sickness has reached an advanced stage.

What to do when mountain sickness occurs

As it is not likely that oxygen flasks will be carried, the only thing to do is to seek a lower level at once.

There are drugs such as Pervitin or the similar Maxidon which increase endurance by up to six to eight hours; afterwards, however, when these last reserves are exhausted, a complete physical and psychical collapse may result. This happened to Siegi Low on the descent from Nanga Parbat in 1962, resulting in his death. Accordingly, the best advice is to consult your own doctor if you are contemplating using such drugs, which can be obtained only on prescription.

Regarding the use of alcohol: it has a slight transitory 'gingering-up' effect in the case of exhaustion or mountain sickness; after the effect has worn off exhaustion sets in more rapidly and to a greater degree.

Opposite: Tired girl ramblers. If they want to get nice and brown they should put on an anhydrous preparation for protection against ultra-violet rays.

Sunburn (glacier burn)

At 1500 metres the solar radiation is double that in the valleys, and in winter it is four times stronger. If we add to this reflection from new snow (it reflects up to 90 per cent of the light), old snow (60 per cent) or ice (25 per cent), the radiation high up is very much greater than in the plains. The droplets of water of which mist is composed also have a dangerous 'burning-glass' action.

The face is least affected by the sun's rays; if, however, larger portions of the body are exposed unprotected to radiation this can lead to severe burning which will require medical attention.

Protection against sunburn
Like the rest of the anatomy, the skin has to get used to the height and the radiation. As soon as a protective brown tan has formed, the main danger is past.

Reinhold Messner from South Tyrol after his return from Nanga Parbat, looking many years older.

Snow blindness

Anhydrous preparations for protection against excessive light assist in preventing sunburn but must be applied before the commencement of extensive radiation and should again be applied if removed by sweating. It is worth mentioning here that clothing made of artificial fibres (perlon, nylon, etc.), in contrast to wool, form no protection against ultra-violet rays.

Symptoms of sunburn

Slight sunburn is regarded as burning of the first degree. Symptoms are reddening of the skin, swelling and sensitivity to touch. The second stage is reached when blisters appear on the skin, usually not until some hours later.

As the skin of the lips is particularly sensitive, the first burning takes place here. There is danger of infection and severe suppuration.

The third stage causes damage to the deeper-lying layers of skin resulting in destruction and loss of patches of skin.

So long as no blisters have formed, avoidance of further exposure to the sun's rays is a sufficient precaution. If, on the other hand, blisters or severe damage to the skin have occurred, medical attention must be sought.

This is the result of strong solar radiation on insufficiently protected eyes. Basically, it is a form of sunburn of the mucous membranes, the retina of the eyes. Snow blindness is often due to snow glasses not having been worn in mist or haze, for such conditions of luminosity are positively dangerous, a fact which is often underestimated by many mountaineers.

Protection against snow blindness

The eyes must be protected from the short-wave ultra-violet rays which occur with strong solar radiation or reflection from snow and glaciers. Sun glasses supplied with side protection should be worn, a fact frequently overlooked when purchasing.

Snow glasses should be bought for their light-absorbing properties rather than because they are the latest fashion. By 'absorbing'

This climber, sitting on the Chogo-Lungma Glacier in the Himalayas at an altitude of about 4700m, is wearing sun glasses and a face protector, the best possible protection against solar radiation.

119

Camp at 5000 metres in the Himalayas. Always wear a hat, preferably a light-coloured one with a wide brim, when exposed to strong solar radiation at great altitudes.

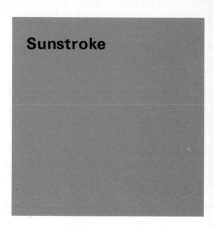

Sunstroke

is meant that not too many of the dangerous rays are allowed to penetrate. Absorption of 85 per cent or over will guarantee complete security from snow blindness. Good glasses have Neophan lenses; better are those with Umbral lenses.

The glasses must fit well and sit properly on the nose so that they do not fall off at every movement. There are special glasses for mountaineers, provided with a cord so that they cannot fall off and get lost. Although snow blindness rarely has after-effects, it is not wise to leave the eyes unprotected for long periods.

Symptoms of snow blindness

These are sometimes disclosed at once, but in the main not for several hours after being exposed to the rays.

The first signs are a slight flickering before the eyes, followed by tears, swelling and reddening of the retina, a burning feeling and, finally, but much later, a sensation as though there was sand in the eyeballs. When this last stage is reached the cure is several days' rest in a darkened room.

This is damage to the brain caused by solar radiation and is due to direct action of the reddish-yellow rays of the sun's spectrum on the unprotected head or nape of the neck. This causes bleeding from the fine brain vessels.

The most treacherous thing about sunstroke is that no external symptoms become visible until the exposure is long past. According to the Swiss doctor, Rudolf Campell, a severe attack can bring on amnesia lasting for days or weeks, give rise to a temperature of up to 105·8 °F (41 °C), followed by unconsciousness and death, if medical treatment is not sought.

Precautions against sunstroke

Prevention is the best precaution. Always wear a hat in the noonday sun or when exposed to its rays. The best type is one with a brim or a cap; this, however, will hardly afford protection to the neck. The headgear should not be made of artificial fibres as these afford less protection against radiation.

Dr Gottfried Neureuther, doctor of the Bavarian Mountain Rescue Service and head doctor at the Garmisch-Partenkirchen infirmary, strongly advises that a hat should be worn even if the sky be overcast, 'as injury from radiation can occur without exposure to the direct rays of the sun if there is a thin cloud or mist layer present'.

Symptoms of sunstroke

The recognition of the first signs of sunstroke is extremely important, for if they are diagnosed too late the consequences dealt with at the beginning of this section will ensue.

The first symptom is lassitude, followed by headache, occasionally attacks of vertigo and vomiting. This can be cured by the application of a cold wet compress, headache remedies and sleep.

Should the attack get worse with vomiting, rapid pulse, cramp and high fever, the victim must see a doctor at once.

In the advanced stages, particularly with a high temperature, it is not possible for a lay person to distinguish between sunstroke and heatstroke.

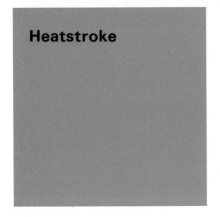

Heatstroke

Owing to insufficient giving-off of heat from the body when undergoing strenuous exercise in hot, moist and calm weather, a build-up of heat takes place if the clothing does not allow free access to cooling airstreams.

Heatstroke can take place just as well in the plains as on the heights; the body temperature rises to over 104 °F (40 °C). In contrast to sunstroke, heatstroke may occur after a delay of from one to two days. At the first sign of an attack the expedition must be broken off at once.

Precautions against heatstroke

The clothing must be airy and permit reasonable regulation of the body heat. At best the air should flow over the body from top to bottom, as this affords the best possible aeration.

Fluid lost by sweating must be replaced by drinking, with the addition of cooking salt or salt tablets. Let cool water run over the arms, temples and torso.

Symptoms of heatstroke

Once again, rapid recognition is of great importance, as an advanced stage of heatstroke can lead to collapse.

First symptoms are palpitation of the heart, very red face, headache and lassitude.

The advanced stage is distinguished by general indisposition and vomiting, followed by collapse. Even if a long rest is taken following an attack and the descent started, there remains the danger of heart trouble. For this reason periodic halts must be made. Finally, two to three days of absolute rest are necessary.

Nightfall

When it gets dark there is always the danger of getting lost and falling, so as far as is possible a place of shelter must be found or a bivouac established.

Naturally, if the route is obvious, climbing can continue after dark if due care is taken, preferably with the aid of a lamp.

If the climber is able to cope with the difficulties likely to be met with, the ascent can continue with the help of a headlamp. Climbing of this nature, however, should be practised beforehand.

It should be stated here that climbing with a lamp might be taken by the Mountain Rescue Service to constitute distress signals.

Even on very easy ground, the rope should invariably be used when climbing at night. It is very dangerous to follow the course of a glacier after dark. Apart from the use of a lamp, the ordinary safety precautions employed in mist should be applied (see page 105).

Roping-down on unknown terrain should never be attempted after dark. However, if the situation demands it, then two knots should be tied at the end of the rope about 1½ metres apart. A karabiner must be attached to one side of the doubled rope, which is fastened to the harness. If the man abseiling should fall or cannot find a stance when he comes to the end of the rope, he remains suspended from the top knot by the karabiner attached to the harness and can utilize the lower knot like an abseil loop to support his weight. In other words, he cannot fall from the rope.

Opposite: Bivouac on the Grand Pilier d'Angle on Mont Blanc. Protection against cold by bivouac sacks. Articles of equipment are tied on.

Right: Comfortable bivouac in a down sleeping sack on the north face of the Grosse Zinne (direct route). The climber (Werner Bittner) is wearing a headlamp. All equipment is well tied on.

The bivouac

It is often necessary on a big climb to sleep out on the mountain. This may be on the way up, on the summit or on the descent. It is usually known before the start of a climb if a bivouac is likely and the necessary preparations will be made.

Many guidebooks or descriptions of routes enumerate bivouac sites, so that the climbing programme can be adjusted accordingly. In general, a site for a bivouac should be sought about an hour before nightfall. Under no circumstances go on climbing until darkness sets in with the possibility of spending the night slung from étriers.

Skiers and walkers should also be prepared for a night in the open, for it may not always be possible to reach the hut or refuge before dark owing to injury or losing the way. Thus, the climber must carry a bivouac

Opposite: Construction of snow
shelters and igloos, taking
advantage of a depression.

Abseil in a 'Dülfer chair' with a
stirrup at the end of the rope.

sack with him. It is a completely
erroneous assumption that this
article of equipment should be
taken along only on serious
ascents; even in a short thunder
shower one can keep dry under
the impermeable perlon cover.
Many a mountaineer owes his
life to the shelter afforded him
by his protective bivouac sack
during a prolonged break in the
weather.

Choice of a bivouac site

This should be protected as far
as possible from avalanches and
falling stones, reasonably comfortable, dry and out of the wind.
If one is caught out on a glacier
or névé at nightfall, a safe place
should be sought in a bergschrund or a crevasse, naturally
with the adoption of proper
precautions. A suitable site can
also be contrived in drifted snow
on a slope or a depression in the
ground where there is no danger
from avalanches and where a

snow cave can be dug without
much expenditure of energy.
Never bivouac in gullies or
gorges; in rain they can all too
easily become raging torrents.
The possibility of danger from
lightning should also be taken
into account.

Construction of a bivouac

A bivouac in rope slings requires
no construction; in such a case,
suitable belays must be provided
followed by the creation of a
'rope railing' to support the
climber during the night.
Lothar Brandler and Dieter Hasse
used hammocks in bivouacs on
the occasion of their conquest of
the southwest face of the Rot-
wand in the Rosengarten range.
These are attached to pitons and
are very comfortable, according
to Hasse.
Quite recently bivouac tents have
come into fashion, for which,
naturally, sufficient space must

overhand knot

about 1m

figure-eight knot

be available. This, of course, is always the case on glaciers. There are also bivouac sacks in the form of a tent; these do not require any internal support as they are designed for hanging up. Generally speaking, however, most bivouacs consist of the customary sack. If the bivouac site is in any way exposed or there is any risk of the climber sliding off the mountain, personal belays must be used.

If at all possible, the bivouac should be protected by a stone wall — 18 inches high will do — from the prevailing wind. Seating accommodation made of rock slabs will form a protection against the cold ground, a fact which is often underestimated. During the night the cold coming from the earth can be largely eliminated by lying on rucksacks or ropes, which can also compensate for the unevenness of

the ground. In hard firn ice it will take more time to dig out a hollow space with the iceaxe. In new firn snow which has set and is somewhat hard on the surface, it is an easy matter to cut out squares which can be used as a windbreak when resting. Good snow houses (igloos) can be dug out of winter snow with an avalanche shovel.

Although in calm weather the bivouac tent may be used instead

Nightfall at the so-called 'Austrian Bivouac' at the foot of Schchara (Caucasus). Down clothing as a protection against cold.

of such snow structures when a night has to be spent in the open, some tips for the building of these structures are worth having. In order to stop thaw water dripping onto the occupants, the vault of the igloo must be in the shape of a pointed arch. The floor must be higher than the entrance so that the cold air will not infiltrate and the thaw water can flow out. A thaw-water channel should be constructed around the edge of the floor inside.

Insulation layers (ropes etc.) must be provided. Knowledge and practice in the construction of bivouacs and shelters is necessary before trying them out in earnest.

Behaviour in a bivouac

I can remember many a bivouac when we slept right through the night and did not stir before the rays of the rising sun woke us up. I can also recall nights spent in the open when our perlon sleeping sacks were shaken by a raging snowstorm and condensation water soaked our down sacks and froze them, and nights when the uncertainty of the way ahead and the bitter cold would not allow us to sleep a wink. These nights on the mountain were all entirely different, but none of them was romantic as far as I was concerned.

There is more to be done than just sitting or lying down and pulling on the bivouac sack, as is frequently assumed.

If the situation of the bivouac site permits, one should lie down (well belayed), for in this manner the circulation of the blood is improved and it is easier to rest. Keep as close together as possible so that the loss in heat is reduced to a minimum. Although lying close together reduces the heat loss, it may also restrict the circulation of the blood if one is in a cramped position.

Usually one slips into the sack while lying down, so that the head is at the opening. The perlon cover should be tied tight round the neck to prevent the heat escaping. When in a sitting position, the sack is pulled on over the head and the feet pushed into the rucksack. The personal belay should, unless it is introduced through the air ventilation slit, be long enough to stop the sack being raised too much.

To prevent freezing or super-cooling, one must ward off the cold by movement, reciprocal massage, hot drinks, etc. Anybody who goes to sleep in such a situation may never wake up.

If possible, clothing should be changed before settling in. If the bivouac is not one-hundred per cent safe from stonefall the helmet should be worn all night. Tie on all articles of equipment such as rucksacks, ironmongery, iceaxes, etc. If using torches or lanterns, be careful that they cannot be seen in the valley and be mistaken for distress signals.

Quite a respectable fug can be made in the sack with a candle; guard against allowing the flame to get too close to the texture of the sack.

Hazards due to equipment

Can we discuss hazards due to the equipment in a book dealing with hazards of mountaineering? In my opinion, yes. Let us consider a fall and the build-up along the chain of belay, which extends from the fallen man to the belayer via the harness, the rope and karabiner and pitons. Like every other chain, the chain of belay is only as strong as its weakest link.

If the above-mentioned links remain sound it will not go further than a fall on the rope. On the other hand, if one of the links fails a catastrophe might occur. This is a demonstration of how hazards due to equipment are bound up with the hazards of mountaineering in general and must be considered together. It was a personal experience which induced me to write this chapter. On a practice climb, a friend of mine who was directly above me fell owing to a pear-shaped karabiner breaking when he placed his foot in an étrier attached to it.

An 11 mm 'kernmantel' rope broke after a fall of 30 metres on the north face of the Viererspitze in the Karwendel range. Fortunately I was attached to a second rope. This occurred, however, in 1959, and since then ropes have improved considerably.

When screwing in a corkscrew-type ice screw on the Mönch in the Bernese Oberland, it broke off where the spiral joins onto the rear piece. I did not find this out until I tried to pull myself up by it and it broke away.

Since 1950, the UIAA (Union Internationale des Associations d'Alpinisme) has concerned itself with mountain equipment and has established the 'International Commission for Safety Equipment' with some degree of success. For example, there exists a UIAA test certificate for rope and karabiners. Any rope which corresponds to the standards required by the Stuttgart Research Institute or the Schools of Technology of Vienna or Toulouse is awarded the UIAA certificate. This will eventually apply to pitons and climbing helmets.* However, standards must be established before this can happen, and in the case of helmets it may take some time.

Since 1968, a so-called 'safety commission' has been formed

* In Britain, the Equipment Sub-committee of the British Mountaineering Council has issued important circulars on pitons (Nos. 454 and 603) and helmets (No. 591) among other matters. As regards helmets, the BMC recommends that BS 4423:1969 covers the requirements for mountaineering use. Information on BMC recommendations may be obtained from the British Mountaineering Council, 26 Park Crescent, London W1N 4EE. The BMC magazine, *Mountain Life*, also contains Equipment Sub-committee reports from time to time.

The rope as a connecting link between the climbers and an important link in the safety chain. (Northeast face of the Lenz-spitze in Canton Valais.)

within the framework of the German Alpine Club. This commission, which is composed of active mountaineers, seems at the moment to be more productive than the UIAA. For a very long time the hazards due to equipment were accepted as an unavoidable evil. The last decade has shown, however, the great dangers to which they exposed the mountaineer.

The climbing rope

Originally, this article of equipment served as the only means of safety and, in fact, it is the principal safety device today; it is also used, however, as a means of progression. The demands attaching to this naturally lead to compromises in manufacture without, however, setting aside the first demand of all, namely the safety of the persons entrusted to it.

What does the UIAA Test Certificate guarantee?

Every single rope, i.e. a rope which will guarantee complete security in case of a fall under ordinary conditions of usage, must fulfil the following conditions in order to gain the UIAA test certificate.
1. Must sustain two falls of 80 kg and a fall factor of 1·78 (see below) without breaking.

2. Must sustain a maximum impact force of 1200 kg on the first fall.
No climber should use any rope other than those which have the UIAA certificate.

The fall factor

From this is estimated the severity of a fall. It consists of two components:
1. The height of fall.
2. The length of rope under load by reason of the fall.
This fall factor is calculated by the ratio of height of fall to length of rope run out and cannot be greater than 2. For example, if the leader is 5 metres above the second man, he can fall 10 metres free. Therefore the height of fall (10 m) divided by the length of rope run out (5 m) gives a fall factor of 2. If, on the other hand, the leader has knocked in intermediate pitons, the fall will be less severe and the fall factor less than 2.
The more pitons used, the less the fall factor, and by the same inference the less severe the fall, the less the 'jerk load'.

The 'jerk load' (Fangstoss)

This is the sudden stress which is imposed on the pitons and karabiners and also on the bodies of the fallen leader and his second. If the elasticity of the rope is small, there will be a high 'jerk load', and if the elasticity is

great there will be a low 'jerk load'.

Construction and practical properties of the rope

Claus Benk, rope expert and head of the Edelrid Co., writes as follows:

'There are three main types of rope construction, of which the rope with the separate core (core and sheath, or kernmantel, ropes) is the most practical. Spirally woven (or "cabled") ropes having the lay of the strands at an oblique angle to the longitudinal axis of the rope are now very little used, mainly owing to the disturbingly high elasticity with low tensile strength (a characteristic of rubber).* One good thing about kernmantel ropes is the relative freedom from kinking as compared with the twisted ropes, which are very apt to kink, especially if large quantities of pitons are used. The cored rope with separate sheath consists of two separate elements, as the name implies. The internal

---

* In Britain, however, the BMC considers satisfactory cabled ropes which still conform to the British Standard 3104. The thickness recommended for rock climbing with a single rope is No. 4 ($1\frac{3}{8}$ in. circumference) with a strength of 4200 lb. Other thicknesses are No. 3 ($1\frac{1}{4}$ in. circumference), 3500 lb; No. 2 ($\frac{7}{8}$ in. circumference), 2000 lb; and No. 1 ($\frac{5}{8}$ in. circumference), 1000 lb.

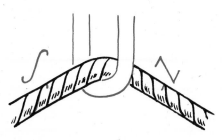

Left: S-twists to the left and Z-twists to the right of the karabiner where the rope is running at an oblique angle. If the rope is removed from the friction effect of the karabiner, the twists will straighten out; otherwise kinking will occur.

Right: Kinking, a hazard due mainly to improper handling of the rope.

load-bearing core is firmly enclosed by the sheath. The sheath has several important duties and contributes towards the successful handling of the rope. It gives the necessary stability of form to the rope and protects the all-important core, the load-carrying portion, from abrasion and other harmful external influences. This two-part construction offers the possibility of changing the surface structure and therefore the gripping propensity of the rope. Well-constructed ropes today are required to exhibit good gripping propensities even when new. At the same time, the surface should not be too rough so that it runs over rock only with difficulty, nor should it be excessively liable to abrasion.

Gripping propensity of the rope

'With increasing length of use the capillary fibres of the rope gradually break owing to the abrasive action of the rock. This produces projecting ends of fibre on the surface which contribute to the gripping propensity.

'The more grip there is, the better will the second be able to hold a fall, abseiling will be steadier and the paying-out and hauling-in of the rope easier.

Suppleness of the rope

'This should seldom vary under any weather conditions, even rain or ice. To achieve this, the textile raw material from which the rope is manufactured must absorb no, or very little, water. Perlon meets with this requirement to a large extent but drops of water lying between the separate fibres will cause a wet rope to become slightly stiffer at temperatures below freezing point. However, compared to the earlier hemp ropes this is of little consequence.

'The more pliable a rope is, the easier it runs through karabiners and the easier it is to manipulate.

Manipulation of the rope

'The different practical properties of the rope can be combined under the term "manipulation". As well as gripping propensity and suppleness, the tendency towards kinking is of considerable importance.

'On modern climbs, where a large number of pitons are employed, kinking may be a serious problem especially if only one karabiner is attached where a piton extension sling or a short series of karabiners would be preferable. If the rope runs at an oblique angle over the edge of a karabiner, "S" twists are formed before, and "Z" twists after, contact with the karabiner [see sketch]. This twisting effect would immediately subside if

Hauling up equipment during the first ascent of the southwest face of the Fourth Salbit Tower. In the foreground the twisted sheath of the rope is plainly visible.

the rope could be freed from the friction effect of the karabiner, otherwise kinking will occur.

'Kinks in the rope which occur during climbing should be straightened out by unroping at the next convenient stance. Kinking can to a large extent be prevented by using the double rope technique and the so-called piton extension slings.

'Coiling the rope can also be a source of kinking. The conventional rope ring method (knee and foot) brings about a partial twisting motion in the rope because, owing to the great length of the rope, the ends are not free to move. As long as the rope is coiled in the same way and direction (i.e. on the ground), very little twisting occurs. This can be recognized by the so-called ridging of the sheath. If one looks along the surface in the direction of the longitudinal axis, ridges can be seen running round

135

the rope, in fish-bone pattern. If this pattern runs parallel to the axis of the rope it will be free of twists and kinks.

'Rébuffat employs the French method, whereby the rope is doubled at the middle mark and then coiled.

[It has more than once been stated that nylon or perlon ropes may melt and break owing to thermal action. This applies, however, only where a moving rope runs across a standing rope under load, in which case there may be a severe heat build-up in the standing rope, sufficient to melt it. It is important to state, though, that it is only the standing rope and not the main or active rope which may be affected. In view of the exceedingly rapid movement of the active rope, the heat is dissipated along its whole surface and it is impossible for the heat generated by friction to penetrate right through to the core. Signs of melting will, at the most, appear only on the surface of the rope. The sheath takes on a protective function similar to the heat shield on a space capsule.]

'There is no cure for mechanical damage due to rope in contact with rope, or in the case of a fall if the rope runs over sharp edges of rock. It is clear that thicker ropes are more advantageous in such situations. A considerable factor of safety is

American climbers use only one rope for progress. Webbing slings are used in place of piton extensions and stirrups.

offered by the double rope technique, employing two ropes.

What is the life of a perlon rope?

'The question of the length of life of a perlon rope is a difficult one to answer. It depends upon a variety of factors, as follows:

1. Frequency of use.
2. Type of rock.
3. Construction of rope. (Spirally woven ropes wear out quicker than cored ropes with a protective sheath (kernmantel ropes).)
4. Treatment of rope.

'These numerous and often very different influences make it impossible to provide exact statistics of the length of life of a rope.

'At the moment, unfortunately, there is no research data available concerning the efficiency of used climbing ropes. Thus, the following statistics can give only a general approximation:

Length of life of UIAA-tested ropes:

 9 mm double rope
   500 run-outs (rope lengths)
11 mm single rope
   250 run-outs (rope lengths)

'If one estimates that the average climber has an average of 125

When climbing on fairly easy terrain (west ridge of the Gimpel, Tannheimer mountains) the rope sheath is scarcely subjected to any friction. If properly handled there is little danger of kinking.

Artificial climbing on rock. On 'the greatest roof in the world' (north face of the West Zinne), webbing slings are used in place of rope extensions. There is thus less friction on the rope and less liability to kinking.

Webbing slings as an aid to climbing. In the USA they rope up round the stomach as a matter of course. This is the most sensitive part of the body.

run-outs per annum, the life of a 9 mm double rope would be from three to four years, and an 11 mm single rope about two years. After these times have elapsed, the ropes would no longer be safe. The 11 mm rope is in this sense only restricted in its "safeness" when used as a single rope. Engineer Dr Ernst Kosmath has the following to say about the length of life of climbing ropes: "The general consensus of opinion usually credits the length of life of a rope as from 100 to 150 days, whereas in actual fact it is only a fraction of this figure, i.e. about 19 to 37 days." *

'A rope that has been involved in a serious fall (fall factor 1·0 and higher with a fixed belay) is no longer fit for use.

Double or single rope?

'According to the UIAA classi-fication, ropes are divided into two groups: double ropes and

* The BMC has carried out further tests in the light of Dr Kosmath's work and has concluded that mountaineering *ropes* of nylon or perlon would normally be expected to have a safe life of not less than 100 days, provided they are not damaged. In the case of *slings*, however, 100 days is a maximum and they should be discarded by then.

The webbing sling knot. This knot does not slip under load, in contrast to the overhand, figure-of-eight and fisherman's knots.

single ropes.

'In order to fulfil the UIAA demands, rope diameters of at least 7·5 mm for the double rope and about 10·5 mm for the single rope are necessary, according to the present technical standards. Practical demands lay down the diameters with a lower limit of 8·5 mm and an upper limit of 11·5 mm.

'If in determining the diameter one excludes the possibility of a fall and relies merely on the practical qualities — manipulation, gripping propensity, volume, easy insertion in pitons — the optimum diameter can be reduced to about 10 mm.

'As a significant compromise between the various demands, the figures for the double rope have evolved from 9 mm diameter for the double rope to 11 mm for the single rope. If one examines the dynamic performance of these ropes and compares it with the demands of the UIAA, it is established that the double rope has considerably greater reserves of safety than the single rope, provided it is used in accordance with double rope technique.' So much for Claus Benk.

Resistance of ropes to cold

Here there is no material data. Rope makers, however, are optimistic on this point: 'The good qualities of the Edelrid rope are maintained even under extreme winter conditions.' Fritz Zintl, spokesman for the German Alpine Club, states: 'Cold and wet can reduce the breaking strength of perlon ropes by about 30 per cent. The more often a rope is frozen, the greater is the reduction in breaking strength.'

Care of the rope

Recent research has brought to light that heat and damp produce a certain state of sensitivity in polyamide material, which causes it to deteriorate.

Wet ropes should always be stored under dry and airy conditions, never in a damp and warm atmosphere. Never under any circumstances dry out a rope before a fire. It should be washed in a hand-warm solution of fine detergent.

Strength of knots at webbing slings

The Safety Committee of the German Alpine Club has made the following report which could be of vital importance to mountaineers: The well-known knots, such as the bowline, figure-of-eight and fisherman's knot, should not be used with webbing slings as they slip under load. The only safe knot to use is the so-called 'webbing sling knot', a form of overhand knot (see illustration above).

139

The climbing belt or harness

The great advantages of a climbing belt have been indicated in the section on falls on rock (page 23). There is, therefore, nothing more to be said on the necessity of wearing harness. As practically all climbing belts conform to the test conditions of the UIAA, they afford the necessary safety conditions.

The rope must be fastened directly to the chest loop of the belt, using the customary knot. From a safety standpoint one should not attach it by means of a karabiner, except on glaciers when a karabiner with maximum breaking strain is employed.

The wider the belt, the more protection it will afford to the body.

Hard edges or rear knots can also become unpleasantly restrictive. The belt should be placed from 2 to 4 inches below the armpits, and the chest loops must not overlap but be up to 2 inches apart.

When abseiling, the belt has special advantages at stances. A short line is sufficient to belay oneself at a stance; without a belt this would become a very tedious operation. A good belay is also afforded (see page 25).

Karabiners

After the rope, the karabiner is the most important article in the safety chain and is absolutely indispensable for the climber. As it does for ropes, the UIAA provides certificates of excellence for karabiners which meet a minimum load of 2200 kg (4820 lb) on the major axis (keeper closed) or 1200 kg (2640 lb) with keeper open; the sustainable load on the minor axis must be at least 600 kg (1320 lb). This standard applies equally to screw and non-screw karabiners and is suitable for all normal purposes including running belays and attaching the main rope to the body.

According to the latest data supplied by the German Alpine Club Safety Committee, the theoretical maximum load to which a karabiner at a static belay can be subjected is about 3000 kg. However, only about a third of all karabiners offered for test approach this breaking point.

With most karabiners the breaking strain is given in kilogrammes. Here a word of caution is necessary. The breaking tests carried out by the Safety Committee (Hermann Huber, Pit Schubert) showed that five samples of the Rosskopf Alu 2000 (tested by the manufacturer up to a breaking load of 2000 kg) gave an average figure of less than 1700 kg, and five samples of the ASMü-Steel 3400 (small size) gave not quite 3000 kg. It should be stated that with each sample of the last type a rope sling (11 mm cored rope with high 'jerk load') broke, after which there was no further test.

As a contrast to this, the 1800 kg Bonatti-Steel karabiner maintained an average breaking load of 3052 kg until a rope sling broke.

Which karabiners stand up to maximum loads?

The following table is based on breaking tests carried out by the German Alpine Club Safety

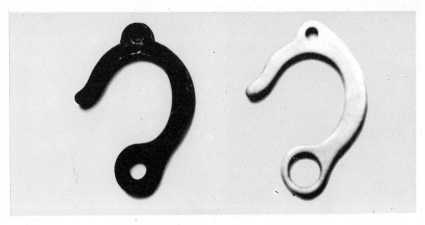

Hazards due to equipment. The model of the 'fiffi' hook on the left has been found to break under load behind the upper eye, which is impossible in the case of the model to the right.

Committee. The samples were all taken from the sales stocks of the two leading Munich mountain sports equipment stores. The ASMü samples were tested up to the breaking point of one rope sling only. Karabiners with a breaking load of below 1300 kg (the old oval iron karabiners, according to the Safety Committee) could not match up to a fall factor of 0·25 and were therefore dangerous.

Karabiners below the maximum breaking load

As already stated, only a third of all karabiners obtained from commercial sources correspond to the maximum breaking strain of 3000 kg identified by the German Alpine Club. What can one do with the remaining, mostly lighter types? They can be used without further ado as auxiliary or progressive karabiners, but never for belaying at a stance or anywhere where a higher fall factor is to be reckoned with. Always use karabiners of maximum breaking load at a belaying point or beyond it and where pitons are more than 20 feet apart. It is not advisable to clip two ropes into the same karabiner as this would increase the 'jerk load'.

Type	Average value (kg)	Maximum value (kg)	Minimum value (kg)
Stubai-Alu-2200	2875	3010	2740
Allain-Alu-2800	2970	3010	2890
ASMü-Steel-3400 (small size)	2972	3180	2860
ASMü-Steel-3400 (large size)	3042	3180	2920
Bonatti-Steel-1800	3052	3180	2910
Stubai-Steel-5000	5497	5620	5375

The dangerous screw karabiner

The threaded sleeve which screws over the locking clip is assumed by many climbers to guarantee unlimited safety, but it adds nothing to the strength of the karabiner (which will break at the pin in the gate). The screwed portion is there only to prevent the clip from opening. This can be useful in rescue work etc., and also for abseiling in the so-called 'karabiner chair'. Many instruction manuals recommend the use of a screw karabiner for roping up with a climbing belt — but make sure first that the total strength of the karabiner is adequate. . . . Let us consider the following case. During the course of a German Alpine Club karabiner breaking test, the threaded screw broke, the clip opened and the test weight of 80 kg fell to the ground. This 80 kg is equivalent to the weight of a human body of about 160 lb.

Rock pitons

The piton is the end of the safety chain. At present there are no UIAA certificates for pitons and, unlike karabiners, no indication of the breaking load (at the eye). It would be helpful if, as regards their application, pitons were distinguished as belaying or progress pitons, for what is the use of having UIAA standards for ropes and karabiners if pitons are not in accordance as regards their strength? For, without doubt, the piton is the weakest link in the chain, as tests carried out by engineer Heinrick Opitz from Erlangen on the static breaking strain have shown. Mountaineers owe a great deal to Opitz regarding safety of equipment.

Pitons subjected to a maximum breaking load

Their use corresponds to that of karabiners (see page 140). However, as long as there is no UIAA standard for the breaking load of the eye and pitons are not differentiated, the climber is dependent upon the information supplied by the equipment salesman.

Which pitons hold maximum loads?

Maximum load is taken to be a breaking load of 3000 kg, which is the same as that imposed by the Safety Committee on karabiners tested by it.

Although the loading of pitons is not in the same category, the data supplied by Opitz can be regarded as representative and is appended in the following table in kilogrammes.

As Opitz had only a testing machine of up to 3000 kg at his disposal, the limiting values (short or long) of the ASMü pitons could not be determined.*

* In Britain, tests carried out by Dr Griffin at the National Engineering Laboratory have shown that well designed high-tensile alloy steel pitons have much greater holding power than those made from malleable steel or iron: in horizontal cracks 2000–5000 lb (as against only 400–4200 lb for soft steel) and in vertical cracks 800–4600 lb (as against 200–3200 lb).

The oval iron karabiner seen below
the right foot does not stand up to
a fall factor of 0·25 and should
therefore be excluded from the
'ironmongery'.

Type	Breaking strength (kg)
Salewa safety piton (long)	2800
Stubai 'knife-blade' ring piton (long)	2985
Stubai 'knife-blade' ring piton (short)	2985
Stubai angle-iron ring piton (long)	2985
Stubai angle-iron ring piton (short)	2985
Stubai ring piton (longitudinal-diagonal, long)	2985
Stubai ring piton (longitudinal-diagonal, short)	2985
ASMü 'knife-blade' Fiechtl piton (short–long)	3000
ASMü angle-iron Fiechtl piton (short–long)	3000
ASMü Fiechtl piton (longitudinal-diagonal, short)	3000
ASMü Fiechtl piton (longitudinal-diagonal, long)	3000

Ice pitons

Hazards due to the ring piton

Common opinion is that the ring is very apt to break away at the seam of the weld; however, Opitz states that this may not be so. But if the weld seam comes to rest at a sharp edge of the piton or karabiner when under load (and in practice this cannot always be controlled), a considerable decrease in the strength of the ring must be expected. This disclosure inspired Opitz's collaborator, Fritz Sticht, to invent a triangular 'ring' in which the seam is at the apex of the triangle and therefore, owing to its position, thought to be stronger.

Straightening of bent pitons

Usually the inserted piton is recovered by the second man and taken along with him. They are mostly in a bent condition and have to be restraightened — nearly always in the cold state. We are grateful to Heinrich Opitz for his valuable statistics on the strength of cold bent and cold wrought pitons. He found that the breaking strength of the piton blade sank to a third of its normal value when bent to and fro five times in the cold state at an angle of bend of 70 degrees.

Compared with rock pitons, the breaking strength of ice pitons (at the eye) is of less importance for safety. For example, what is the use of the customary pitons with a static breaking strength at the eye of 3000 kg if, when subjected to sudden or constant load, they break out of the ice more easily than a screw piton with a breaking strain of only 1200 kg?

Moreover, belaying media on ice are rarely exposed to loads such as occur with rock pitons, for free falls on ice are extremely infrequent.

The most effective belaying medium on ice has been found to be the long Sticht ice screw, but as it has a static breaking strength of only 2400 kg at the eye, intermediate belays must be interpolated in order that the maximum falling force involved does not exceed 1200 kg. This means the insertion of ice screws

Descending the Piz Bernina. No iceaxes with wooden shafts are equal to extreme loads when climbing on ice.

at 8, 12, 18 and 27 metres above the stance when using a 40-metre rope. If Marwa ice screws are employed, the intervals can be much less. In order to obtain maximal security it is naturally important to know the correct angle at which to insert the screw, with regard to the presumable direction of stress. This should be as follows: ice piton at right-angles, ice screw less than about 135 degrees.

Iceaxes

In the spring of 1971 the German Alpine Club Safety Committee published a report on breaking tests on iceaxe shafts which concluded that 'no iceaxe shaft made of wood can stand up to extreme stresses on ice'.

The test material consisted of eight new axe shafts made of ash, hickory and Rexilon (glued wood), also eight used shafts

145

Fritz Sticht with his brake plate, affording dynamic belaying. This means that the belayer is subjected to only a comparatively slight jerk if his companion should fall.

of ash which had been used on ice for periods of from 100 to 1200 hours.

How can the average climber know whether a shaft is relatively good or relatively bad? Pit Schubert proffered three golden rules in the Safety Committee's action report for 1969–70:

1. Wood in which the run of the fibres is uniformly rectilinear will give higher strength.
2. The closer together the growth rings in the wood, the greater the strength.
3. The less the wood is subject to rot (usually invisible), the greater the strength and toughness.

But how on earth can one determine whether the wood is rotting or not? Schubert has got an answer to this too. Take your penknife and dig out a chip from the shaft. The shorter the chip the more rot is present, resulting in reduced strength and toughness. However, no sports-shop salesman is going to be very pleased to see a potential customer digging around in the shafts of his axes. Until, therefore, manufacturers produce some breaking-load values or guarantees of

Antiquated equipment. A winter ascent of the southeast face of the Riffelkopf (Wetterstein mountains) fifteen years ago.

some sort, it is difficult for the climber to be able to lay his hands on a relatively good ice-axe shaft. At the moment one has to depend on ash, for about 95 per cent of all axe shafts are made from this wood. Alternatively, a metal-shafted axe may be used, such as that put on the market by Salewa in the summer of 1971.*

The BMC also advises that snow-anchor plates (aluminium plates of up to 10 by 12 inches) – or 'deadman plates' – provide more reliable belays than iceaxes on steep snow since they can sustain a much greater load if correctly placed.

* In Britain, metal-shafted axes (e.g. the MacInnes axe) have been available since the early 1960s and are preferable to wood-shafted axes on account of their greater strength. The BMC in 1970 recommended that climbers purchasing wooden-shafted iceaxes should seek to ensure that the shafts are made of hickory of grades AA or A, of BS 3823:1965.

Conclusion

The research into articles of equipment continues, particularly as regards safety measures. That is very gratifying, but at present climbers are lucky if they can obtain 100-per cent security from a single link in the safety chain. In his article entitled 'Was Halten Karabiner?' ['What is the strength of karabiners?'], which appeared in the Yearbook of the German Alpine Club for 1969, Pit Schubert, an aeronautical engineer, had this to say: 'In other technical domains where similar loads are encountered and men's lives are at stake, a 300- to 600-per cent safety factor is expected'. This is a serious statement, for the alpine equipment sector is very far from attaining such standards.

Within the scope of this book it is not possible to consider other articles of equipment such as the climbing helmet. The present helmet gives no guarantee what-ever against injury to the skull or cervical vertebra. Either the shell is too weak or, on the other hand, it is too strong and transmits too much force to the cranium. Who knows, however, how much the human cranium will withstand? The UIAA will eventually produce a specification for helmets but it may take a long time. How is industry going to react to such a specification? It will mean entirely new construction methods. Until this happens the climber will have to content himself with the scarcely cheerful fact that a bad helmet will protect the skull better than none at all.

There is no doubt whatever that climbing accidents will always happen. A man will never be completely proof against his own shortcomings, the weapons of nature or the failure of some technical article of equipment. One can, however, restrict these hazards to a minimum — and that is the purpose of this book.

Glossary

Abseil bollard A bollard or spike to which the abseil rope is attached.

Abseil harness Support for the thigh made of webbing. Can be combined with the climbing belt.

Abseil piton Piton through the eye of which the abseil rope is threaded.

Acclimatization Physical adaptation to great heights.

Aiguille Needle, with particular reference to the needle-shaped peaks in the Mont Blanc Massif.

Basalt Neo-volcanic intruded rock, greyish black or black in colour.

Bivouac To sleep out.

Bivouac sack Wide sack of perlon or similar material, open at one side and having a ventilation slit. It has no poles or struts and can sleep one or two or two to four persons as in a sleeping bag. Alternatively a plastic bag may be used.

Cairn Heap of stones erected to mark a route, also sited on summits and trigonometrical points.

Chlorous schists Slightly weathered schist containing chlorite (salt of the chlorous acids).

Cirque or corrie An extensive, deep, rounded hollow with steep sides and back, formed through erosion by glacier ice.

Climbing skins Strips, originally of seal-skin, now of nylon plush, attached to the running surface of skis to facilitate climbing.

Core and sheath rope (kernmantelseil) Consists of two parts, the rope core (the load-bearing component) and the rope sheath enclosing the core, which protects it against abrasion or other external forces.

Couloir French word for gully, ravine or wide cleft.

Crampons Sets of spikes which have eight to twelve points and are attached to the boot soles by means of straps. They facilitate safe progress and climbing on snow and ice.

Crusted snow Hard snow with a superficial crust, formed from a variety of conditions.

Detritus Matter produced by detrition (wearing away by rubbing), such as gravel, sand and silt.

Dolomite Sedimentary rock composed of calcium and magnesium carbonates.

Dolomites Limestone Alps in South Tyrol and Italy. Named after the discoverer of the rock, the Frenchman Dieudonné de Gratet de Dolomieu.

Eckenstein technique A technique invented by Oscar Eckenstein for climbing on steep ice, using ten-point crampons instead of the now generally used twelve-point type.

Eruptive rock Rapidly cooled and solidified magma, such as basalt etc.

Étrier A type of ladder for holdless pitches.

Fall line Vertical line connecting a high point on a mountain with a lower one, e.g. in the fall line of the summit.

Fel(d)spar Kinds of crystalline white or flesh-red mineral.

Ferner West Tyrolean name for glacier.

Foliation Splitting of rocks into laminae.

Glissade Sliding down in a standing or sitting position on steep snow or névé slopes.

Gneiss Crystalline rock. Partly primitive igneous rock, partly primitive metamorphic sedimentary rock, it has a distinct parallel structure of very variable mineral content and very variable density.

Granite Fully crystalline igneous rock.

Graywacke Dense, coarse- to fine-grained sedimentary rock.

Green schist Schist formed from igneous rock under pressure.

Ground avalanche Wet old snow avalanche.

Hammer iceaxe Shorter version of the usual axe fitted with a hammer head.

Harness or climbing belt
Harness made up of rope lengths or webbing fastened round the chest and to which the rope is tied.

Iceaxe Axe with a blade and a pick for cutting steps in ice and snow.

Iceaxe (short) A short iceaxe fitted with a blade and hammer head.

Ice screw Spiral or corkscrew-type belaying medium for use on ice.

Ironmongery Word used by the climbing fraternity to describe equipment such as pitons, karabiners, etc.

Jumar Artificial method of holding oneself on the rope. Easier to manipulate than the Prusik knot.

Karabiner Oval metal ring with a clip on one side which is closed by the action of a spring. It is attached to the eye or ring of a piton and holds the rope which runs through it.

Karabiner chair Abseil technique in which the rope runs through a karabiner attached to the harness and finally over the shoulder.

Karabiner knot A karabiner used in conjunction with a Prusik knot.

Katabatic wind Wind flowing down from higher regions (such as föhn).

Ledge Very narrow, flat or sloping step on a steep face.

Length of rope The length of the climbing rope is usually 120 feet or 40 metres (130 feet). It is used as a measure to determine the length of rope between climbers. With the 40-metre rope, after allowing for belaying and roping-up to the harness, there will be only about 35 metres left for climbing.

Lichen Small plants which adhere to the rock surface.

Line 4–9 mm — thick perlon line, used for abseil slings, piton extensions, Prusik knot slings, knotted rope slings, etc.

Mica schist Schist distinguished by its rich mica content. It is light, weathered, laminated and soft.

Mountain Rescue Service
Formed in each alpine country to render assistance to victims of mountain accidents, often in association with the police. In Britain it is organized by the Mountain Rescue Committee.

Perlon Nylon possessing remarkable strength in wet or dry conditions. Also has high elasticity, high resistance to chafing and low moisture absorption.

Piton Metal spike, with an eye or ring, driven into cracks in rock or ice and used as a means of belay and progression.

Plateau Extensive level area in high mountains.

Plutonic rock Solidified deep down in the earth from magma.

Porphyry Volcanic rock containing potassium felspar of great geological age.

Prusik knot Sliding friction knot used for attaching a sling to the standing rope. Grips tightly when under tension and can be slid upwards when freed from tension. The Austrian, Dr Karl Prusik, invented the knot for repairing violin strings and later on adapted it for climbing purposes.

Pulley Method of hauling up articles, injured men, etc.

Regelation Refreezing of ice after melting under pressure.

Ring piton Rock or ice piton having a welded ring in place of the customary eye.

Rock slide Simultaneous fall of large masses of rock.

Rope railings Backrest at stances or a fixed rope placed by the leader on traverses etc.

Rope slings Can be used as a substitute for pitons when attached to small pinnacles or rock bollards.

Roping up Attaching the rope to the chest or harness.

Running belay Rope loops used as a substitute for pitons with karabiners and placed round projecting rocks.

Sandstone　Rock of compressed sand.

Scale of difficulty　Ranges from I to VI (easy to extremely difficult) for free climbing on rock. From grade III onwards the grades are subdivided into a lower (−) and a higher (+) section. Artificial climbing is graded from A0 to A4. If expansion pitons are used a small 'e' is added, e.g. A3e. According to Hintermeier, the scale of difficulty on ice can also be graded from I (up to an angle of about 30 degrees) to VI (over 75 degrees).

Scree　Slope of fragmented rock, caused by weathering.

Screw karabiners　Karabiners having the clip protected by a threated screw-on sleeve to prevent involuntary opening.

Shoulder belay　Method of belaying whereby the belaying rope runs over the back, shoulder and under the arm of the belayer. Has limited application owing to its low safety factor.

Slabs　Rock at 30–70 degrees of incline.

Stirrup slings　Fixed to the rope, usually by means of a Prusik knot, so that a fallen climber can support his own weight.

Traverse　To cross a face, either obliquely or horizontally.

Tree line　Boundary determined by climatic conditions above which trees do not grow.

UIAA　Abbreviation for 'Union International des Associations d'Alpinisme'. An alliance of national mountaineering organizations.

Webbing slings　Special nylon webbing material used in place of line. It comes in different widths, such as 16, 20 and 25 mm. Although these slings weigh little they have a relatively high strength.

Wooden wedges　Used in wide cracks which would not hold the ordinary piton.

Useful conversions (approximate)

1 metre	=	3·28 feet
100 metres	=	328 feet
1000 metres	=	3281 feet
2000 metres	=	6562 feet
3000 metres	=	9843 feet
4000 metres	=	13 124 feet
5000 metres	=	16 404 feet
1 cubic metre	=	35·31 cubic feet
1 litre	=	1·76 pints
1 kilogramme	=	2·20 pounds

Rope sizes

40 metres	=	130 feet
$1\frac{3}{8}$ inches circumference	=	11 millimetres diameter
1 inch circumference	=	8 millimetres diameter
$\frac{7}{8}$ inch circumference	=	7 millimetres diameter
$\frac{5}{8}$ inch circumference	=	5 millimetres diameter

Bibliography

Compiled by Louis C. Baume,

Gaston's Alpine Books

This is not a complete bibliography of technical books; it is a selection of the principal works for the general reader which have been published recently in book or in article form. For quick reference, the bibliography has been divided into nine sections. As techniques and scientific knowledge have developed and expanded so rapidly in recent years, this selection — with perhaps two or three exceptions — has been limited mainly to books and journals published since 1960. This does not imply that certain earlier books are no longer relevant; they may well be, for the fundamental principles of mountaineering remain unchanged: it is our understanding of them and our capacity to cope with them which have evolved.

References to more abstruse subjects, such as oxygen equipment and its use, have been omitted. Many of the books listed, particularly those in the first section, deal with matters relevant to other sections too. Books marked with an * contain important bibliographies of additional and often more specialized works in their particular subjects. Most of the items listed below are still in print and are available in Club Libraries or from specialized booksellers such as Gaston's Alpine Books (134 Kenton Road, Harrow, HA3 8AL, England) and others.

AAC = American Alpine Club
AJ = Alpine Journal (British)
CAI = Italian Alpine Club
DAV = German Alpine Club
ÖAV = Austrian Alpine Club
RGS = Royal Geographical Society

General instruction

Blackshaw, A., *Mountaineering*, sub-titled 'From Hill Walking to Alpine Climbing', rev. edn 1970.

Brower, D., *Manual of Ski Mountaineering*, Sierra Club, USA, rev. edn 1969.

Disley, J., *Tackle Climbing this Way*, new edn 1968.

Dixon, S. M., *Rock Climbing*, Know the Game Series, 1964.

Federated Mountain Clubs of New Zealand, *Safety in the Mountains*, 5th edn 1961.

Francis, G., *Mountain Climbing*, Teach Yourself Books, 2nd edn 1964.

Greenbank, A., *Instructions in Mountaineering*, 1967.

Langmuir, E., *Mountain Leadership*, Central Council of Physical Recreation, 1969.

Manning, H. (ed.), *Mountaineering: The freedom of the hills*, The Mountaineers, USA, 2nd edn 1971.

Murray, W. M. and Wright, J. E. B., *The Craft of Climbing*, 1964.

Rébuffat, G., *On Ice and Snow and Rock*, 1971. Written and pictorial, translated from the French.

San Diego Chapter, Sierra Club, *Basic Mountaineering*, USA, 3rd edn 1970.

Styles, S., *Arrow Book of Climbing*, 1967.

Williams, Sqn Ldr P. F., *Camping and Hill Trekking*, 1969.

Wright, J. E. B., *The Technique of Mountaineering*, 3rd edn 1971.

Young, Geoffrey Winthrop, *Mountain Craft*, 7 editions in all.

Avalanches, snow

Atwater, M. M., *The Avalanche Hunters*, USA, 1968.

Fraser, C., *The Avalanche Enigma*, 1966.*

Journal of Glaciology. For advanced studies.

Roch, A., 'An approach to the mechanism of avalanche release', *AJ*, vol. 70, 1965.

Roch, A., 'Avalanches', *Mountain World*, 1962–1963.

Roch, A. and Fraser, C., 'How to estimate avalanche danger', *AJ*, vol. 72, 1967.*

Seligman, S., *Snow Structure and Ski Fields*, 1936.

Swiss Federal Institute for Snow and Avalanche Research, *Lawinenverbau im Anbruchgebiet*. Published in English as *Avalanche Control in the Starting Zone*, Colorado State University, USA, 1962.

United States Dept of Agriculture Forest Service, *Snow Avalanches: A handbook of forecasting and control measures*, 1961.

Equipment

Alpine Journal. A special section devoted to equipment and kindred subjects is included in each volume as from vol. 74 (1969).

Brower, D., *Going Light — With backpack or burro*, Sierra Club, USA.

Crew, P., *An Encyclopaedic Dictionary of Mountaineering*, 1968.

Meldrum, K. and Boyle, B., *Artificial Climbing Walls*, 1970.

Mountain Magazine. Equipment notes feature regularly in most numbers.

Schubert, Pit, 'Was halten unsere Karabiner?' DAV annual, 1969.

Ice and rock climbing

Bisaccia, M., 'Un contributo ai problemi dell'assicurazione', *Rivista Mensile del CAI*, February 1972.

Casewit, C. and Pownall, D., *The Mountaineering Handbook*, USA, 1968.

Chouinard, Y., 'Climbing cracks', *Journal of the AAC*, 1970.

Contamine, A., 'Ice climbing', *Journal of the AAC*, 1969.

Germain, F. (ed.), *Alpinisme moderne*, France, 1971.

Greenbank, A., *Instructions in Rock Climbing*, 1963.

Lovelock, J., *Climbing*, 1971.

Mazzenga, G., *Sécurité en paroi*, 1967. Translated from the Italian.

Mendenhall, R. and J., *Introduction to Rock and Mountain Climbing*, USA, 1969.*

Nock, P., *Rock Climbing*, 1963.

Robbins, Royal, *Basic Rockcraft*, USA, 1971.

Smith, G. A., *An Introduction to Mountaineering*, USA, rev. edn 1967.

Sturm and Zintl, *Sicheres Klettern in Fels und Eis*, Germany, 1969.

Sutton, G., *Artificial Aids in Mountaineering*, 1962.

Unsworth, W., *The Book of Rock Climbing*, 1968.

Medical and survival

Adam, Col. J., *A Traveller's Guide to Health*, RGS, 1966.

Bhattacharjya, B., *Mountain Sickness*, 1964.

Brendel, W., 'Höhenakklimatisation und Höhenkrankheit', DAV annual, 1965.

Edholm and Bacharach, *Exploration Medicine*, 1965.*

Gardner, A. W. and Roylance, P. J., *New Essential First Aid*, 1967.

Hillman, Dr H., 'Cold, the killer in our mountains', *Mountain Life*, No. 2, 1972.

Hultgren, H. N., 'Treatment of high altitude pulmonary edema', reprint from *Journal of the AAC*, 1965.

Outward Bound Trust, 'Exposure', reprint of article from the *Climber* magazine, 1963.

Ward, Dr M., 'Man and the mountain environment', *AJ*, vol. 74, 1969.*

Ward, Dr M., 'Frostbite', *AJ*, vol. 76, 1971.

Washburn, Bradford, 'Frostbite'. Its definition, treatment and prevention. Reprint from the *Journal of the AAC*, 1962. (Originally in the *New England Journal of Medicine*, 1962.)

Wilkerson, J. A., *Medicine for Mountaineering*. Handbook for treatment of accidents and illness in remote areas. Published by The Mountaineers, USA, and reprinted 1969.

Nutrition

Bunnelle, H., *Food for Knapsackers*, Sierra Club, USA, fully revised edn 1971.

Durig, A., 'Über Bergsteigerernährung', DAV annual, 1952.

Lewis, H., de Jong, A. and Harris, J., 'British sledging ration development', Symposium on Antarctic Logistics Report, National Academy of Sciences, Washington, USA, 1962.

Other sources. The Appendixes of most official books on the major Himalayan or other expeditions contain valuable information on food (e.g. Hunt's *Ascent of Everest*, 1953; Ullman's *Americans on Everest*, 1965; Bonington's *Annapurna South Face*, 1971).

Rescue and accidents

AAC, 'Accidents in North American mountaineering', annual reports and findings, published since 1948, USA.

AJ vol. 74 (1969) and AJ vol. 75 (1970) both contain a number of articles and notes by various contributors.

Bridge, L. D., *Mountain Search and Rescue*, New Zealand, 2nd edn rev. 1961.

Central Council of Physical Recreation, *Safety on Mountains* (a booklet), 8th edn 1972.

Hartley, H. K., 'Survey of British mountain accidents, 1959–1968', *AJ*, vol. 75, 1970.

Her Majesty's Stationery Office, *Mountain Rescue*, training handbook for the RAF Mountain Rescue teams, 1968.

James, R., 'A comparison of mountain rescue stretchers used in Britain', *AJ*, vol. 73, 1968.

Katz, C., 'The rope held but . . .?', *Journal of the Mountain Club of South Africa*, 1969.

Kirkman, N. F., 'Advances in rescue equipment in Britain', *AJ*, vol. 75, 1970.

MacInnes, H., 'Our electronic age – but rescue dogs are still unbeatable', *Mountain Life*, No. 2, 1972.

Mariner, W., *Mountain Rescue Techniques*, ÖAV, 1963.*

Mountain Rescue Committee, *Mountain Rescue and Cave Rescue* (a booklet), rev. edn 1972.

Weather

Bowen, D., *Britain's Weather. Its workings, lore and forecasting*, 1969.

Gatty, H., *Nature is Your Guide*, 1960.

Hoinkes, H., 'Der Wolkenhimmel in den Alpen', ÖAV annual, 1950.

Robertson, D., 'Just how temperate *is* Britain's climate?', *Mountain Life*, No. 2, 1972.

Sutton, P. G., *Understanding Weather*, 1960.

Other sources. More advanced works on weather can be found in the *Journal of the Royal Met. Society*, publications of HMSO and articles in the *Geographical Journal* (RGS). But weather can be very local, and useful information can be found in the contents or appendixes of many books on particular mountain ranges or peaks.

Sundry

Les Alpes - Die Alpen. Journal of the Swiss Alpine Club. Articles dealing with all the above sections appear from time to time in this excellent publication. They are published in either German or French.

The Explorer's Journal. A scientific quarterly published in New York, USA. A useful source of reference.

Hints to Travellers, vol. 2. Covers organization, equipment, scientific observation, health, etc. Published by the RGS.

The Polar Record. The Journal issued by the Scott Polar Research Institute frequently contains articles relevant to mountaineering, e.g. 'Crevasse rescue' by E. W. K. Walton, vol. 8, 1957.

Index

On the Mer de Glace
(Mont Blanc Massif),
below Montenvers.

Climbers on the
'Yellow Ridge'
of the
Kleine Zinne.

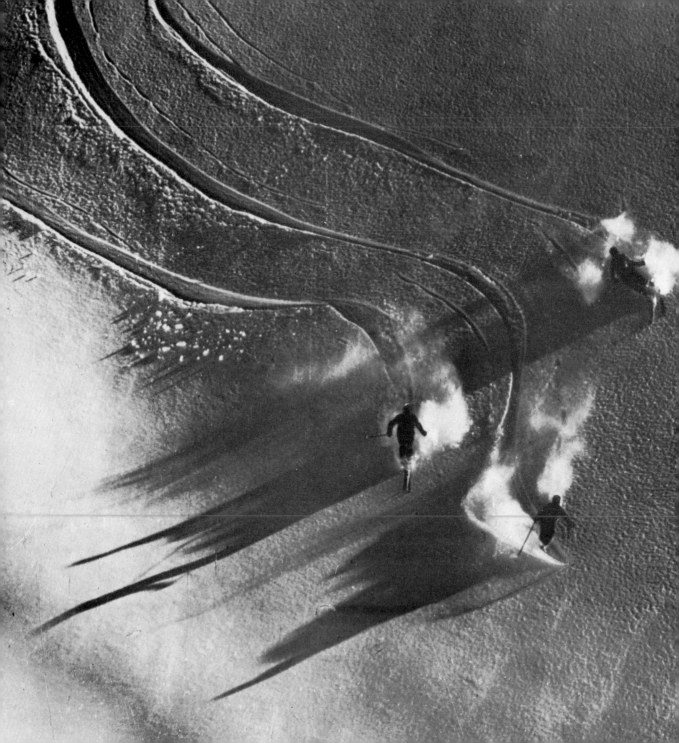

Illustration
acknowledgements

Well equipped . . .

Baumgartner, Albert 53, 99
Bavarian Red Cross 25, 64
Behrisch, Charlotte 49
Brandler, Lothar 125

Cleare, John 24, 89, 158
Cooper, Ed 130

Desmaison-Film 65
Dumler, Helmut 16, 22, 49, 84, 102, 110,
   137, 141, 143, 146(II), 148
Dyhrenfurth-Film 114

Fed. Institute for Snow and Avalanche
   Research 33(II), 42, 61
Feneberg 86

Gczychi, Peter v. 119, 120
Gorter, Jürgen 54, 108
Grassler, Helmut 36
Grob, Willi 135

Hanschke, Thomas 15, 76
Heckel, Vilém 67, 79, 128
Homberger, Ruedi 88
Höpperger, Heinz 33

Kerner, Uwe 115
Klier, Heinrich 47
Klopfenstein 41
Köfferlein, R. 101

Lapuch, Kurt 58
Lindel, Rolf 105
Lindner, Rudi 20, 83, 123
Loderbauer, Hannes 39
Lüthy-Bavaria 45

Messner, Reinhold 118
Meyer-Blankenburg 81

Muhr-Anthony 10

Pauli, Gerhard 69

reobild Hartig 61
Robbins, Royal 138
Rother Rudolf Panorama

Schmied, Hans 49, 161
Scholz, Georg 35, 92
Schott, Karl 117, 145
Schymik, Hans 93
Scott, Douglas 21, 136, 137
Seibert, Dieter 85
Spanner, Richard 53
Storto, Walter 61

Thorbecke, Franz 60
Trachsel, Hans Peter 90

Wagner, Hans 38, 72, 98
Weis, Helmut 15, 78
Winkler, Jürgen 9, 14, 37, 52, 57, 68, 69,
   70, 71(II), 73(II), 74, 76(II), 77(II),
   79(II), 82, 87, 90, 100, 103, 104, 105,
   132, 139
Wünsche 10

Zawadzki, Ryszard 124
Zeiss-Ikon 160
Zingerle 127

unknown 27, 37, 155